Falling Through the Ice

Falling Through the Ice

The Path of a Zen Methodist

J. D. Hiestand

RESOURCE *Publications* • Eugene, Oregon

FALLING THROUGH THE ICE
The Path of a Zen Methodist

Copyright © 2014 J. D. Hiestand. All rights reserved. Except for brief quotations in critical publications or reviews, no part of this book may be reproduced in any manner without prior written permission from the publisher. Write: Permissions. Wipf and Stock Publishers, 199 W. 8th Ave., Suite 3, Eugene, OR 97401.

Resource Publications
An Imprint of Wipf and Stock Publishers
199 W. 8th Ave., Suite 3
Eugene, OR 97401

www.wipfandstock.com

ISBN 13: 978-1-4982-0016-5

Manufactured in the U.S.A.   09/12/2014

Scripture quotations marked (NIV) are taken from the Holy Bible, New International Version®, NIV®. Copyright © 1973, 1978, 1984, 2011 by Biblica, Inc.™ Used by permission of Zondervan. All rights reserved worldwide. www.zondervan.com The "NIV" and "New International Version" are trademarks registered in the United States Patent and Trademark Office by Biblica, Inc.™

Scripture quotations marked (KJV) are taken from the Holy Bible, King James Version, Cambridge, 1769.

Excerpt from *Borderland* © 1987 by Marilyn J. Carwin. Used by permission of the author.

Who else could I dedicate this work to except the two women who have filled my life with joy, pushed me towards excellence and kept me from falling too hard?

My mother, Barbara Hiestand and my wife, Vivian Hiestand.

Events and people in these stories are taken from my memories and experiences. A few names have been changed in order to protect the privacy of those individuals, and I have occasionally modified reality somewhat in order to, as W.S. Gilbert wrote, "add verisimilitude to an otherwise bald and unconvincing narrative."

Table of Contents

Prelude | 1

Part I: Themes | 11
    Chapter 1: Zen | 13
    Chapter 2: Nature | 24
    Chapter 3: Music | 33
    Chapter 4: Christianity | 39

Part II: Dissonance | 47
    Chapter 5: Family & Zen | 49
    Chapter 6: Art & Authenticity | 57
    Chapter 7: Relationships & Religion | 65
    Chapter 8: Nexus I | 76

Interlude | 87
    Chapter 9: The Choke | 89
    Chapter 10: Credo | 94

Part III: Counterpoint | 105
    Chapter 11: Passages | 107
    Chapter 12: The Guilt List | 114
    Chapter 13: Death By a Million Flea Bites | 123
    Chapter 14: Nexus II | 136
    Chapter 15: One Road Home | 145

Postlude | 159
    Chapter 16: Starbucks | 161
    Chapter 17: Beginner's Mind | 165

Acknowledgments | 171

Bibliography | 173

Prelude

I AWOKE CONTEMPLATING THE passing of an old friend; it was a disturbing way to start the day. I wondered if I might be under the illusion that his fate was in my hands—or maybe, it wasn't. This was assuming, of course, that he wasn't already gone, obliterated—or maybe, he was. The truth was I didn't actually know if Alan was still around or not, and I realized if I chose to I could go on not knowing for quite some time. So the question that really disturbed me that morning wasn't whether or not Alan was still alive, it was whether or not I wanted to know.

As I lay in bed trying unsuccessfully to sort things out, the sun rose in an unhurried fashion over Long Scraggy Peak. It lazily overflew the town of Buffalo Creek, then made its way upward, crossing over the North Fork of the South Platte River until it reached my bedroom windows with gold, piercing, high altitude light. On most days, my wife and I would simply draw the curtains closed and sleep in, proving we could be just as unhurried as the sun. But on this particular Wednesday morning we were too anxious to sleep in, I for reasons I suspect my wife Vivian did not share. So we rose, made our tea and coffee, and watched the squirrels and birds vie for the mountain of bird seed that we had poured into the feeder the night before. Days at our cabin near Bailey are often like this, except for the rising early part, and often no real activity begins until 10 or 11 a.m. Afternoon naps are required after a casual lunch, and by four o'clock we would look at each other in astonishment wondering how the day had gone by so quickly without us accomplishing anything. This was followed by that guilty/wonderful feeling that we really didn't need to accomplish anything anyway: the earth was still turning and the squirrels were still hungry.

Prelude

Vivian and I had been fortunate enough to get a couple of days rest at the cabin before we were obliged to attend the Annual Conference of the United Methodist Church in Denver, an hour or so away. This annual confab of Methodist clergy and laity in the Rocky Mountain Conference would culminate on Saturday evening with a large and formal ordination service, where new clergy would be officially ordained as Elders in the United Methodist Church. Vivian and I were two such new clergy, and some of our anxiety stemmed from the number of hoops we anticipated having to jump through before the big ceremony on Saturday. We had both served provisionally for two years as ministers and had managed all of the previous hoops successfully, but still . . . For this reason, Vivian was understandably anxious about the future, while I remained inexplicably anxious about the past.

The cabin in Bailey is our refuge. Even though it sits in a little subdivision, the lots are large and scattered amongst the conifer forests in a way that makes us feel isolated in the mountains, as if we were miles away from everywhere. The quiet seems intense when we first arrive, but it becomes soothing after a few days as our spirits realign to the natural world around us. Below us Deer Creek purrs softly on its way to the confluence with the North Fork of the South Platte, while crows and ravens, magpies and chickadees, hawks and even the occasional Golden Eagle circle overhead. It seems like the first real home I've had in years, since after leaving home at nineteen I had moved around frequently in California, Washington, Oregon and Colorado. It was ironic that we had at last found a place of rest and repose at the same time we were joining an organization famous for its itinerant clergy. So we clung to Bailey stubbornly even as we moved around the Rocky Mountains from church to church. No matter where we served, we felt we always had a place to come home to; a place where we could rest our minds, souls and bodies, and most often accomplish the sacred nothing.

On that Wednesday evening, after lunch and naps, Vivian realized we had nothing in the fridge for dinner, and would I pleeeeease drive down to Conifer and get something: chicken or steaks to barbeque would be good. Conifer was 20 minutes away, but it was the closest town with a grocery store, so I got in the car and snaked my way through the back roads until I arrived at Highway 285, where I turned north and headed into 'town.'

I had barely pulled on to the highway when my cell phone rang and it was Vivian. A friend had called and suggested that they have an old-fashioned gals night out at the Cutthroat Café in Bailey and they couldn't

Prelude

wait for me to get back with the groceries, and I wasn't invited anyway 'cause I wasn't a 'gal,' and so I should just get whatever I wanted and cook it up for myself when I got back 'cause they were going to be a while.

OK. Might as well continue on into town.

As I drove along the highway, my thoughts returned to the passing of my old friend Alan, which inevitably led me into a persistent journey metaphor. As I pulled into the parking lot of the Safeway, I thought aimlessly about how many times I had driven this route, actually and metaphorically. On the eve of ordination those drives seemed more than just a little symbolic of the shuttle my life had been on: back and forth between seeking the illusory security of income and career, and seeking deeper meaning in an increasingly vacuous world. Long drives produce odd musings.

Here inside the earthbent edge of heaven,

Within the span of endless sage and sky . . .

My thoughts wandered around until they were unexpectedly far away on Interstate-84 as I tried to piece together my actual and metaphorical journeys. It was a drive that I had taken numerous times between Colorado and the Northwest. Seattle to Colorado Springs, Denver to Portland, over and over again for the last eighteen years. I was conscious enough to realize that my anxiety about the past was related to those journeys, and were somehow tied in with my contemplation of Alan's passing. Why else would they both be bubbling up to the surface now, in a Safeway parking lot? I parked at the far edge of the lot, as far away from the store as I could get, and tried to compose myself and settle my mind before attempting the arduous task of grocery shopping. I closed my eyes and continued to try and sort things out, hoping that the ghosts of journeys past would melt away in the afternoon sun. They did not.

Where clear-eyed dreamers toiled

We wait. Remembering.

Prelude

It is possible to drive from Portland, Oregon to Denver, Colorado in two really, really long days; but most people who have their masochistic tendencies under control will usually drive the 1,600 miles in three long days to accomplish the journey and still arrive at least semi-conscious. It is also a trip that you want to take during daylight, since most of the time you are passing through some of the most scenic country on the earth. Even after having taken this trip dozens of times in my life, I am still in awe of the Columbia Gorge, the Snake River canyons and the Wasatch Mountains. So when my friend Alan called me from Portland and told me that he had found a job in Denver and could I help him drive out, I thought I might enjoy the trip.

I had lived near Portland for almost ten years, but in 2008 I threw my entire life into chaos by enrolling at the Iliff School of Theology in Denver, and my wife Vivian and I packed up or threw away everything we had and moved to Colorado in a twenty-four foot U-Haul. We had previously lived from 1995 to 1999 in Colorado Springs, but had relocated to Oregon to care for Vivian's aging parents. So in moving back to Colorado not only did we change states, again, but I was walking away from a well-compensated career as a computer programmer to become a low-paid pastor in the United Methodist Church. Alan had remained in Oregon and continued his work in high-tech with a job at one of Oregon's famous Silicon Forest companies. Like most of my friends and colleagues, he could not understand why I would make such a radical move, as well as shoot myself in the foot financially, and assumed I would eventually drop out of seminary and come to my senses, return to programming, and retire in the ease and comfort he thought I had earned after 25 years in the computer industry. By June of 2013 I was still shooting myself in the foot and stubbornly remaining in Colorado, and I had arrived at a considerable turning point in my pastoral career: ordination was only a week away.

I assumed Alan got the job in Denver simply for normal financial reasons, but had cooked up the idea of this road trip as a last ditch opportunity to talk me out of my foolishness. One of the reasons I decided to help him drive from Portland to Denver was I thought I ought to let him try. I knew from long experience that I often didn't recognize my own foolishness, and if I couldn't withstand a grilling from the ever-forthright Alan I had no business changing careers.

So one evening in early June I found myself aboard Alaska Airline's 6:35 flight to Portland. After a few hours, the ancient 737 swooped down

Prelude

the Columbia River gorge, flew west past the Portland airport, made a big, loping circle over Washington County, then lined up on the runway lights west to east and landed smoothly on the damp tarmac of runway 10R. I disembarked through a Jetway into Portland's modern, spacious airport, retrieved my luggage and took the shuttle bus to the rental car lot. Alan was the ultimate city dweller and didn't own a car, but had arranged for us to drive the rental all the way to Denver. It was a mid-sized Ford and fairly comfortable, with more than enough room for two guys travelling light. I pulled out of the lot and wound my way out to the freeway. I had taken this route many times when we lived in Portland, which was fortunate considering all the turnoffs and unmarked freeway interchanges that you needed to take in order to get into downtown Portland. It was dark and rainy—not surprisingly—and I couldn't imagine how someone unfamiliar with the peculiarities of Portland driving could have ever found their way into the city. If they were smart I suppose they took a cab or the light rail, but Alan had gone to some trouble to arrange a long distance rental: our home for the next three days.

As I wound over the river and skirted the city in order to go through the tunnel and over to the west side, I wondered again why Alan had gone to so much trouble. His new company had hired movers to get all of his stuff to Denver, and he could simply have flown there himself, taken a cab and moved right in to his new apartment. We had for a time been fairly close, but had experienced the normal drifting apart over the last 5 years since Vivian and I had moved back to Colorado. Was he really so disturbed by the thought of me changing careers and life-direction that he wanted to do some weird kind of intervention, trapped together for three days in a rental car? Did he think I would be desperately unhappy as a pastor, yet somehow fulfilled if I returned to computer programming? Like me, Alan had come into computer programming in the "cowboy" days, when the industry was inventing itself and it was exciting and challenging to go to work every day. But those days had ended when the dot-com bubble burst in the early 2000s, and computer programming became less of a vocation and more of a job. I knew Alan felt the same way about this, but he had decided that relative financial security was more important at our age than fulfillment, while I had decided to limp along financially in search of deeper meaning in day to day life. I also knew that Alan had given up on organized religion a long time ago, regarding it as too shallow and unrewarding and irrelevant

Prelude

to modern times. My problem was that I wasn't certain he was wrong. I needed to be certain.

So there I was on the brink of ordination, 1,600 miles from home and likely to be grilled for three days on the purpose of my life. Would my defenses and arguments stand up? And I was anxious and uncertain about ordination itself. Would this be a defining moment in my life, on the same list with my wedding and the birth of my children, or would it simply be the last of a long series of hoops I needed to jump through in order to be accepted into the clergy club? It might have been easier if I had just ignored all of this and let the whole thing play out unchallenged, but I knew that if I was truly seeking something ephemeral I could not back away from my own doubts and fears.

I turned south off of highway 26 on to 217, then got off the freeway and wound my way through the maze of streets that constituted the Raleigh Hills neighborhood of Portland, finally arriving at Alan's apartment building. In Portland, cars are considered to be a little bit like a malodorous smell, so it took me almost twenty minutes to find a parking place three blocks away. I grabbed my overnight bag and hoofed it up the street in the rain, finally arriving cold and wet like a stray dog at the door of Alan's apartment. I rang the bell while wondering why there wasn't a larger stoop and overhang in a city where it rained all the time, but Alan came promptly to my rescue and ushered me into the apartment.

His apartment was impeccably neat, a talent I had never been able to acquire, though it did have the advantage of being almost entirely devoid of furniture. There was a cot and a chair in the living room, and I could see a few cups in the dish drainer in the kitchen, but the rest was apparently in a moving van on its way to Denver. Alan stood there in the middle of the floor beaming.

"You have a distinctive knock, my friend, but you smell like a rotten fish!"

"And it's good to see you, too! I don't suppose you have a towel?"

Alan went to the kitchen and found a 4"x4" face cloth, which he held out for my inspection.

"Great..."

It was good to see my old friend again. We were about the same age and approximately the same height and build, but he seemed much healthier than I—I really needed to work out more—and his red hair and neatly trimmed beard gave him a distinctive look. He had also acquired the knack

Prelude

of looking really natty in just about anything he was wearing, which on that night was a simple blue polo shirt and Dockers. My button-down and jeans had started out wrinkled in Denver, were not improved by the flight nor the rain, and actually did smell a little like a rotten fish.

He sat on the floor while I occupied the sole chair, and we talked for some time, catching up on life events and common acquaintances. The coffee maker and teapot were on the truck, so we just sipped water from paper cups. But after a while it was clear that both of us were wearying of the superficial conversation, and I finally broke the ice.

"Alan, it's great to see you again, but . . . well, why am I here?"

"To drive with me to Denver, you knucklehead."

"Yeah, I got that. But why didn't you just fly out? Would have been a lot quicker and easier."

His face became serious. "Look, I just wanted to have some time with you, OK? Probably our last time together as you fade away into the numinous realm." He paused to gather his thoughts, then continued, "I used to think you were just like me, that we'd be buddies together and retire together, sit on the porch at the old folk's home and be flatulent together. But something changed and you moved away from Oregon, and a good job with benefits and all. And I sense that you didn't just move away physically; it's like you hopped off the train we were on and jumped on another whose destination is unclear to me. So I need to know: am I a fool for staying on my train, or are you a fool for jumping on to another?"

"Well, that's clear enough! But you know, neither one of us has to be a fool. There are lots of trains and lots of people. And change is inevitable. We can choose it or we can be victims of it, but it's coming all the same. And it's not as if I don't wonder about the train I've boarded sometimes too. But it's the fear of being a fool, rather than the actuality of doing the right thing even if it's foolish, that produces doubt. The trick is learning to ride the train without fear."

"Bravo! Well said. And I concede to you the intellectual argument. Life isn't a zero-sum game, and being foolish isn't our only choice. But . . . I am still wobbly on the emotional argument. Something feels wrong here and I can't put my finger on it. There's something . . . something that's not about fools or choices, or even our control of it . . . whatever *it* is."

We sat for a few moments in a mildly sad silence. I felt what he felt: that even if the intellectual equation added up, the math seemed a little off in the emotional equation. Alan asked the questions that I knew were going

Prelude

to be reiterated over and over again on our long drive. "Why organized religion? Why the Methodist church? I guess I don't really know your life story that well—maybe there's some family connection I don't know about?"

My family history was actually pretty slim when it came to organized religion, but I gamely tried to play the two very weak cards I did have. "Well, I have a very distant uncle, Samuel Hiestand, who was a Bishop in the United Brethren Church back in the 1820s."

"Wow!" Alan exclaimed sarcastically. "He must have been a huge influence on you! Did your mom tell you bedtime stories about ole Uncle Sam the Bishop? And what the heck is the United Brethren Church?"

"Ha-ha. No, I actually only found out about Uncle Sam the Bishop a few months ago, so no actual influence there. And the United Brethren were German speaking Methodists. Like ole Uncle Sam, many started out as Mennonites and for some reason joined with the United Brethren. They merged with the English speaking Methodist Church in 1968; that's how we became the *United* Methodists."

"Ah! I've always wondered . . . not!" He shook his head. "So that's it?"

I pulled out my second, losing, card. "My mother's paternal grandfather was named Arminius Clay Johnston."

"My paternal grandfather was named Payne, and he was, but it didn't make me a sadist."

"Jeez, Alan! The Methodists were, and are, considered Arminians, followers of a sixteenth century Dutch reformer named Jacobus Arminius. He started out as a Calvinist—you've heard of John Calvin, right?—but he had a very hard time with some of Calvin's doctrines, particularly those that limited Christ's atonement. He also had a high theology of grace, considering it unlimited and universal because it springs from God's redemption in Christ, not from human effort. This grace belongs to everyone, even you, Alan, whether they ask for it or deserve it or not."

Alan looked a little stunned. "Well, I guess they did teach you a *factoid* or two in seminary. But even so, did your mom tell you bedtime stories of Grandpa Arminius and his beautiful wife, Grace?"

I was getting a little tired of this. Alan's flippancy was annoying at the best of times, and it had already been a very long day. Nevertheless, Mom had never talked about Grandpa Arminius. I had only found out about him through Ancestry.com at about the same time I found out about ole Uncle Sam the Bishop. Neither had any influence on my life at all, and I don't know why I had even brought them up.

Prelude

"These factoids about the roots of Methodism are actually extremely relevant—in fact, they're crucial to answer your questions—but for me they are much closer to the end of the story than the beginning. There's a lot more you have to know before Jacobus Arminius is going to make any sense, and I really don't want to get launched into all of that tonight. We have three whole days ahead of us for me to tell you about the things that actually did influence me long before I ever heard of Calvin, Dutch reformers and ole Uncle Sam the Bishop."

"OK. I guess I'm asking too many questions anyway. But I have to say, I'm not sure what I'm more frightened of—finding the answers or not finding the answers."

"Well," I said, trying to lighten the mood, "Let's stop looking for them tonight. Nobody can think straight in the dark and in the rain."

"OK," Alan said abruptly, and he immediately rose and walked back to the bedroom, saying over his shoulder, "There's a sleeping bag next to the window. Set your alarm for six o'clock, and we'll be out by seven."

The door to the bedroom closed behind him, and I assumed he would just be sleeping on the floor. I found the sleeping bag and spread it out on the cot, then removed my stinky clothes and put on a dry t-shirt and boxers from my overnight bag. I felt wistful and apprehensive, wondering if I was looking forward to being grilled for three days in Alan's sarcastic fashion. But once I got situated onto the cot and closed my eyes, the long trip from Denver began seeping out of me, and the familiar Portland rain gently sang me into a deep and peaceful sleep.

Part I: Themes

*In the beginner's mind there are many possibilities,
but in the expert's there are few.*

—SHUNRYU SUZUKI, *ZEN MIND, BEGINNER'S MIND*

Chapter 1: Zen

WHEN I AWOKE THE next morning, the rain had stopped and it appeared I would be treated to one of Portland's rare but beautiful condensation-free days. As I sleepily gazed out of the apartment window the sun, not yet visible as it rose to the east beyond the hills, nevertheless caused long streaks of indirect light to appear across the abundant foliage and colorful roses that grew everywhere and gave the city its nickname. When the sun is shining Portland can be one of the most beautiful cities in the world, but it averages only sixty-eight clear days a year, whereas Denver averages a hundred fifteen, a significant difference to someone raised in the California sunshine. And there are roses in Denver, too.

Alan, without benefit of an alarm clock, also appeared, looking natty in his pajamas. Since there was no food in the apartment, we washed up and dressed quickly, getting out the door by 7 a.m. as the sun poked up over the hills. Alan had three suitcases full of his travelling clothes and the last minute items that inevitably get forgotten during a move, and I tossed them into the back seat before returning my overnight bag to the trunk. Alan slipped on his signature aviator dark glasses, looking like a red headed Tom Cruise from *Rain Man*. Portland is a lot like Seattle with a Starbucks located on almost every corner, but out in the suburbs we had to settle for Peet's for our morning lattes and muffins. The drive-through went quickly, and by 7:30 we were on the road.

I reversed my course from the previous evening, heading north on 217 then going east on 26. When you emerge from the tunnel going east, downtown Portland appears like an Arcadian oasis rising out of the forest, as does the sun shining brightly and directly into your eyes. In silence

Part I: Themes

we proceeded over the Willamette River and finally merged onto Interstate-84—our asphalt and concrete conduit for the next two days until we hit Interstate-80 in Salt Lake City.

While driving through the city, Alan seemed satisfied with the quiet, sipping his latte and casually munching his poppy-seed muffin. But by the time we passed through Troutdale, with Mt. Hood towering off to our right and the vast Columbia River flowing to our left, Alan tossed his empty muffin wrapping towards the trash and abruptly picked up where we had left off last night.

"Alright, so tell me about this ordination crap."

I bit my tongue, being all too aware that the trip would be filled with colorful and irreverent language. If I challenged him on it now, the rest of the trip would be filled either with manic shouting or sullen silence. I preferred something resembling a conversation, and so I ignored the tone.

"Well, a week from today, after writing innumerable papers, presenting myself at innumerable interviews, not to mention the acquisition of an expensive Master of Divinity degree, and serving for four years as a pastor of some form or another, the Bishop will lay her hands on me, pronounce the historic words, and I will be an Ordained Elder in the United Methodist Church."

"You know," Alan said, "I didn't really understand a word of that. You made it clear that Methodism doesn't exactly run in the family, except of course for the highly influential Uncle Sam the Bishop, so I am still puzzled where all of this came from. Wasn't your mom a Zen Buddhist or something?"

"She practiced Zen for a while when I was a kid. I never did, but it's astonishing how those early childhood experiences really shape how you view the world."

"Still, that doesn't really explain becoming a Methodist minister. I've known you for quite a while. You weren't particularly interested in religion when we first met, be it Zen or anything else. In fact, you were as skeptical as I am. Did something happen that I don't know about that has caused you to go all religious on me?"

"Yes, something did happen . . . or maybe, more accurately, some things happened. But it's not perhaps what you're thinking. I wasn't 'saved' by some charismatic evangelical, and I wasn't knocked off my donkey by Jesus like Paul was. Actually, it was a long process that began, I guess, before I was born. In order to understand, you kind of have to know the whole story."

Chapter 1: Zen

"You do realize that I am completely turned off by the church and conventional religion, right? But if I were to become anything, which I won't, I'd be a Buddhist."

"Don't worry, I'm not going to try and convert you to Christianity, or to Buddhism for that matter! And I think the attraction to Buddhism may be more because it is exotic and appears deep, when in fact Christianity can be just as deep even if it doesn't appear exotic. But I have been wondering myself what brought me to this pass, and how things that happened fifty or more years ago have recently become so important, including my mother's dabbling in Zen Buddhism."

"Well, my friend," said Alan as he sipped the last of his Peet's coffee, "I assume there's still plenty of road and sunlight ahead of us. Explain to me how our beginnings precede us, or how we precede our beginnings, or something Zen like that."

My mind's eye turned backwards to those days so long ago, and the events and people who have since passed out of my life. Finally I said, mostly to myself, "God! I wonder what the neighbors were thinking!"

"What . . . ?"

"Had our neighbors been paying attention, they might have noticed a nondescript automobile entering our driveway in the spring of 1966, when I was ten years old. After it entered the driveway it would have disappeared from their view into the plum and cedar trees growing wild to the left, and the chrysanthemum bushes lining the right side of the short driveway that gave our rural/suburban home a great deal of privacy. The neighbors would have had to walk to the head of driveway and peer down the asphalt lane to see where the automobile had parked. Hardly an unusual experience, but they might have been a bit more surprised when the driver emerged from the car. The diminutive oriental man had a shaved head and was wearing flowing maroon robes and traditional Japanese sandals. Such a sight might have startled our nosy neighbors, and even twenty years after the end of World War II the sight of a Japanese man in a California suburban neighborhood might have been alarming. They might have guessed from his attire that the man was a Buddhist monk, but what our neighbors would not have known is that a visit from Shunryu Suzuki to our home was somewhat unusual, but not surprising or alarming. Suzuki-roshi—roshi means teacher or master—was indeed a Zen Buddhist monk, and he had been invited for dinner in our home by my mother. His presence in California during the 1960s changed my mother's life profoundly, and unknowingly laid the foundations of my own spiritual development.

"We lived northwest of San Jose, California, in the small community of Los Altos. In the mid-1950s Los Altos represented the ideal suburban community. Land and homes were inexpensive, lots were large, and my father, Norm Hiestand Jr., was able to purchase a home big enough for his growing family on a large lot near the golf course. He had married my mother, Barbara Johnston, in 1947, and in 1949 my oldest brother Norm was born, followed in 1951 by my sister Harriet, whom we called Hattie Lou in those days. A few years later Dad added an addition on to the home, a swimming pool, and two more kids: my other brother Charlie in 1955, and me in 1956. For the first nineteen years of my life, I never knew anything except the security and freedom of semi-rural suburban living. Surrounded by vacant lots, yet close to the Rancho Shopping center, which I remember fondly as having a world class bakery that created the best chocolate chip cookies a kid could possibly want. Life seemed to have a veneer of predictability, security and conventionality that was the hallmark of a white, middle class family in those times. It was not until I was older that I came to see the rips in that veneer, or that my definition of conventionality was not completely in sync with popular conceptions.

"All of these material privileges were made possible because my father had gotten in on the ground floor of the high-tech industry, which later came to be known as Silicon Valley. In the fifties, high tech pioneering companies like Hewlett Packard were gathered around Stanford University in Palo Alto. My father had received an Electrical Engineering degree from Stanford, and became employee number nine for a new start-up called Varian Associates. When Dad started with them, they were making klystron tubes, an obscure but necessary component of microwave communications equipment. Because this equipment was used by the government, Dad had to travel a lot, including internationally, which later became a problematic lifestyle for him. But in the beginning, it was exciting to be in a cutting edge industry, and Dad used his success to purchase the American dream for his family.

"Dad had started this American dream by wooing and marrying a beautiful and intelligent grad student named Barbara Johnston. My mom had acquired a Master's Degree in Art from Claremont University

Chapter 1: Zen

in Pasadena and married Dad, who had done his undergraduate work in southern California, in 1947. However, my mom bought into, or fell into, the Ozzie and Harriet lifestyle expectations of the 1950s, which dictated that her primary role in society, her primary identity, was that of wife and mother, holding a supporting role for her professional husband. Her artwork could be no more than a hobby, which I think really grated on her rather Bohemian soul. She also inherited a complicated family history. She adored her father, but her mother was controlling and unhappy. After her father died she was obliged to care for her mother, all of which really wasn't in the Ozzie and Harriet script. My grandmother was moved into a little apartment in Sunnyvale, where my parents had lived before moving to Los Altos, but Mom rarely let us kids see her, and when she passed away in 1961 we weren't even allowed to attend the funeral.

"After her father's death in 1954, Mom announced to Dad that she wanted to have more children (to which he prophetically replied, 'Can I finish my drink first?'), and a year later my brother Charlie was born, followed by me the next year. The first hint I had as a child that the perfect suburban veneer might have rips in it came when I was about four or five years old. With four children, my mother was confronted with multiple loads of laundry every day, and I remember walking into our laundry room one day to find Mom sobbing her eyes out as she stuffed another load of laundry into the washing machine. She uncharacteristically yelled at me to 'get out,' and I ran to my room, sobbing my own eyes out. I was certain I had done something wrong to make Mom behave as she had, but I had no idea what. Mom never mentioned this incident, so I didn't either, but oddly I remember it vividly over fifty years later. I guess it qualifies as the first entry on my guilt list, but that little incident exemplifies a vein of deep unhappiness that was starting to surface in the early 1960s.

"Dad chose a different route to escape from the growing unhappiness he felt with his job and family. Social drinking was a way of life in the fifties and sixties, so it only dawned on the rest of us gradually that Dad had a drinking problem. Ultimately, his inability to overcome his alcoholism would cost him his marriage, force him into early retirement and finally contribute to his death. But in the early sixties, Dad would just get 'kinda weird' every now and then. Emotionally distant by nature, he gradually widened the gap between himself and his wife and children, so that we kids could later say with some accuracy as adults, 'I never knew my father.' Sadly, Mom got to witness the transformation of this talented and intelligent man she loved and trusted into the emotional cul-de-sac we knew as children, with no idea how to stop it.

"As early as the mid-1950s, around the time of my birth, Mom must have had some sense that her trajectory through middle-class conventionality was not what she had dreamed of in life, including the growing recognition of a spiritual void. Raised a nominal Christian Scientist—something I discovered only much later in life—she had turned her back on this denomination in particular and religion in general at an early age. At first I think she accepted the notion that the materialism of middle-class living would fill her spiritual void. She perceived the church to be more of a social institution than anything else, which to her meant it didn't really have any spiritual seriousness, a seriousness she craved more and more. When she finally realized that neither church nor materialism could fill this growing spiritual void, she had nowhere to turn in conventional society. Her artwork did provide her with some unspecific spiritual sustenance, and somewhere in the fifties she had discovered a Japanese art form called *sumi-e* which served to partially satisfy her bohemian soul and to fill the importunate spiritual void in her heart.

"Dad chose to fill his spiritual void with gin. Notwithstanding the numbing effects of alcohol, his pain was detectable even by someone as young as I was. Dad had been raised in a religion-less home and by a very domineering mother. Without even the habit of church instilled in him as a child, it never seemed to occur to him to seek God in any form or religion. I don't really think he was an atheist; I think he was just very confused by anything spiritual, particularly when it tried to open up inner spiritual pathways that he had resolutely closed off. He accompanied my mother in some of the more intellectual avenues of exploring Zen Buddhism, but I don't think his heart was really in it.

"Into this dysfunctional American dream stepped the most unlikely of all people: a Japanese Zen monk named Shunryu Suzuki. Suzuki-roshi had arrived in San Francisco in 1959 at the age of 55 in order to take over a Soto Zen temple, and to realize his lifelong dream of teaching Zen to westerners. At that time beatniks and intellectuals in San Francisco had a growing interest in Buddhism, which had sprung up out of San Francisco's long and historic connection with the Orient, and popularized by local writers such as Alan Watts. The presence of a Zen monk in town caused quite a stir within this community. Suzuki-roshi gave a class on Buddhism at the American Academy on Asian Studies that was well attended. He began and

Chapter 1: Zen

ended the class by having the participants sit *zazen* for 20 minutes. He then invited participants to join him for morning *zazen* at his Sokoji temple, which they did in ever increasing numbers.

"At some point in 1964, Suzuki-roshi remarked that if a suitable meeting place could be found, he would be interested in starting a Zen meditation group down the peninsula. Eventually a meeting place was established in a home in Palo Alto, and the first meeting took place in November of 1964. Thursday mornings were chosen because they were convenient for the Stanford student who had organized the meetings. In 1965 the meetings were moved to a home in Los Altos, and it is there that my mother began sitting *zazen* every Thursday morning beginning at 5:45 a.m. For several years Suzuki-roshi led these sessions personally, as well as working tirelessly to establish the San Francisco Zen Center."

Alan finally interrupted "Hold on. You were nine years, maybe ten years old. Were you really aware of all of these stories and histories?"

"No, not really. From my perspective Zen just sort of appeared in my family's life. But later on my mom wrote down her experiences and how she got started with the Zen community.[1] In 1965 she was at a party with some friends and one of them told her there was a Zen Master teaching the practice of *zazen* in Palo Alto one morning a week. Mom had become interested in the subject of Zen through her interest in *sumi-e*. And for a few years she had been attending an annual weekend seminar with Alan Watts on the subject of eastern thought and Zen practice, hosted by friends of ours at their home in Los Altos Hills. But Zen was only an intellectual pursuit up until then, which was kind of ironic considering that Zen is primarily about practice, not thought or belief. She was terrified of actually doing it, but a few months later she learned that the *zazen* group had moved to Los Altos, less than a mile from where we lived, and she began to run out of excuses. Finally in September of 1965 she showed up at the little homemade *zendo* at 5:45 on a Thursday morning for her first session of *zazen*. She met Suzuki-roshi in the foyer before the session began and they nodded politely at each other. After he went in, she removed her shoes and followed him in, and she later wrote these words: '*The minute I stepped into the room, I knew I had come home.*'"

---

1. The full text of my mother's memories can be found online (Chadwick, "Haiku Zendo") in an unpublished history of Haiku Zendo in Los Altos, compiled by David Chadwick and originally edited by my mother, Barbara Hiestand.

19

Part I: Themes

I had to stop for a moment, catching my breath as I remembered Mom's love of that little *zendo* and her adoration for Suzuki-roshi. Alan, unsure of what the silence meant, squirmed for a moment, then said, "Powerful stuff?"

"Yeah. Mom's family history was full of heartbreaking brokenness, and in 1965 she was becoming aware that her own family was not an episode of Ozzie and Harriet. So finding a place that told her heart that she belonged was, yeah, powerful stuff indeed. And yes, she had trouble sitting properly, and never could achieve a full Lotus position, but these were not really hindrances for her in contemplative practice. On that first morning, after sitting a little uncomfortably, the session ended with Suzuki-roshi giving a brief talk, then the small group gathered for a light breakfast. Mom found herself sitting next to Suzuki-roshi and was completely tongue-tied. Suzuki-roshi was, as usual, completely at ease, and began telling her that he had come to America in order to buy a plot of land: a plot of land for his grave! Mom was shocked, Suzuki-roshi was amused, and as far as I can tell they got along perfectly from then on.

"My mother's recounting of her first encounter with *zazen* was typical of the physical difficulties unpracticed Americans had with sitting *zazen*, and Suzuki-roshi was always willing to accommodate the student. The purpose of *zazen* was to cultivate a calm mind to assist in the seeking of enlightenment, not to perform an empty, contortionist ritual.

"As I said, Mom had attended some seminars at a home in Los Altos Hills that belonged to some friends of ours, Win and Helen Wagener. Win and Helen were like an aunt and uncle to us Hiestand kids, and they owned an expansive and architecturally unique home in Los Altos Hills, which they had custom built. The home had been specifically designed to comfortably host private seminars on topics that interested them, and it was here that I have my first memory of Suzuki-roshi. If a physical description of Roshi interests you there are plenty of pictures of him you can find online, but I would not be able to describe him based on my memory alone. What was striking to me as a 9 year old child was his presence. His appearance was highly exotic with his shaved head, oriental features and long robes, but even at a distance you could sense a great depth and calmness within him. His countenance was always friendly, and he paid attention to everything that he did. Unlike most adults, he never condescended to children. When encountering him you got the sense that his spiritual vision was extremely clear. His gaze was not intense like a laser beam, but rather all-encompassing like a large, warm and comfortable quilt. In a way that we would now call typical of a Zen master, he could be extremely practical without any particular concern for outcomes. While I have no doubt that I may have idealized these childhood memories to some extent, I cannot say that I ever saw him fall outside of this Zen calm, or lose the humorous twinkle in his eye. He would draw all eyes in a room towards him not because of his stature (which was diminutive) nor his cleverness (he was always straightforward, and often witty), but because of his presence. He had a habit of dropping unexpected words of wisdom that made you stop and think more deeply about whatever it was you were doing. These were often in the form of a *koan*, which is a puzzle that has no logical answer and is used to expand the mind, but at least in Suzuki-roshi's case these *koans* were usually followed by a laugh and a twinkle in his eye.

"In 1966, Suzuki-roshi expressed an interest in having a typical American meal, so Mom invited him to our home for dinner. Suzuki-roshi had been involved with Buddhism since he was 13 years old, and was a strict vegetarian, a fact well known to my mother. Nevertheless, she served him a traditional American meal of pot roast, which Suzuki-roshi ate up heartily. My sister, who had recently joined in with the Haiku *zendo*, was horrified, but I recall Suzuki-roshi being charming and witty as he politely cleaned his plate. Later, Hattie Lou asked Mom how she could have violated his vegetarianism and served him pot roast, forcing him to eat meat! Mom calmly replied, 'In his culture it would be extremely impolite for him to refuse the meal offered to him, particularly one he had specifically asked for.' As prosaic as this story seems now, it was a classic example of Suzuki-roshi's (and Zen's) emphasis on substance over form, which made an indelible impression on me at an early age.

"The seminars at Win and Helen Wagener's home also included an annual gathering with noted author Alan Watts. Watts was the flamboyant former Episcopalian priest who had taken an interest in Zen in the 1940s, moved to San Francisco in the 1950s to join the faculty of the American Academy of Asian Studies, and published several influential books in his quest to make eastern thought comprehensible to western people.[2] Although I met Watts several times at social occasions and dinners hosted by the Wageners, my best memory of him comes from when I was about ten. In conjunction with a seminar he was doing at the Wagener's home, he

---

2. Probably Watts's most famous book is *The Way of Zen*, originally published in 1957 and now available through Vintage Spiritual Classics.

agreed to do a seminar for children that was hosted in my very own living room at our home in Los Altos. Watts was interested not only in Zen and eastern thought, but in psychology as well. He arrived at our home and set up a flip chart on an easel and began drawing the outline of a human head, and a stick figure of another human inside the head. I was there with my brothers and sister, as well as children from some of the other families attending the seminar at the Wagener's, and we paid rapt attention as the famous man said, 'Now imagine this is your mind, your brain, and inside your brain is a little man who talks to you.' Before he could get out another word on the nature of the ego and the id, my eleven year old brother Charlie piped up, 'But isn't there a little man inside the little man's brain? And isn't there another little man inside that little man's brain?' In spite of his brilliance, Watts was completely flummoxed by Charlie's recursive logic, and the seminar went downhill from there. I never attended one of his adult seminars, but I understand they went much better.

"Many years later I read that Watts did not consider himself an academic philosopher but instead called himself a philosophical entertainer, a description that fits my memories of him to a tee. I can remember seeing him on a rerun of shows he did for KQED TV in San Francisco, bopping himself in the head with something that looked like a nerf bat to demonstrate how a Zen *roshi* would discipline a student. Sadly, even at the age of nine I could perceive he was also a womanizer and a heavy drinker. D. T. Suzuki,[3] the best-known author on Zen at that time, felt Watts's contributions to the western understanding of Zen were dubious at best, but Shunryu Suzuki defended his friend, calling him a 'bodhisattva.'"[4]

"What's a bodhisattva?"

"In Buddhism, once an individual reaches enlightenment, they are released from the cycle of *samsara*, the eternal cycle of suffering in this world, as well as the cycle of reincarnation. This is *nirvana*, the eternal state of self-less-ness, where the self is annihilated and disappears into nothingness. A bodhisattva is one who has reached enlightenment but remains in the cycles of reincarnation and *samsara* for the benefit of all sentient beings. If you have ever encountered someone who appears especially wise, deep and compassionate, they might be a bodhisattva."

---

3. David Chadwick recalls in his biography of Shunryu Suzuki: "When confused with D. T. Suzuki, Shunryu Suzuki would say, 'No, he's the big Suzuki, I'm the little Suzuki.'" (Chadwick, *Crooked Cucumber*, 2).

4. Chadwick, *Crooked Cucumber*, 397.

Chapter 1: Zen

"So, was Watts a bodhisattva?"

"Weeeell . . . who am I to say? Suzuki-roshi thought he was. For me, he ended up being an archetypical example of pathetic human weaknesses combined with an intense striving for the sacred.

"This exposure to eastern thought and vivid characters formed the pattern of religious influence in my home from 1965 to 1971, my sophomore year in high school and the year that Shunryu Suzuki died. Watts followed Suzuki-roshi in death two years later, dying in his sleep aboard his houseboat in Sausalito, passing, as Mom said, 'just the way he wanted to. He couldn't have borne a long illness.' What's important to note at this point is that these experiences were not only formative, they were also normative. Christianity was the peculiar and exotic religion in my home, and was in fact hardly ever mentioned. I was twelve years old before I first entered a Christian church. It was a wedding at a Catholic church, and the religious portions of the service were incomprehensible to me. When the priest mentioned fidelity, Charlie whispered to me, "Does he mean High-Fidelity?" Since stereo recordings were brand new in those days, Charlie and I almost burst trying to stifle our laughter. The church, its rituals and their meanings, were as foreign to us as downtown Ulan Bator. Although in retrospect my feelings were completely unfair to the priest and his church, the Christian rituals I was exposed to seemed empty and meaningless compared to the vibrant presence of Suzuki roshi and his earnest and energetic students. This is even more ironic considering I never practiced *zazen* as a child, teenager or young adult. Nevertheless, my first introduction to religion was one in which the encounter with the Divine was mystical and attained through contemplative practice, rather than an encounter through catechism and scripture filtered by doctrine."

Chapter 2: Nature

THERE IS NOT A more scenic spot in the world than the Columbia Gorge, particularly when the sun is shining and the winds are calm. Several rivers and creeks tumble down through the southern cliffs to create little waterfalls that start by meandering through the moss-laden trees at the top of the precipice before falling down to raucously join the Columbia. These seemed to build up in energy as we travelled east from Troutdale until we passed by Multnomah Falls, a much larger spray of cascading water that justifiably attracted a large swathe of tourists. From there we passed through the little towns of Cascade Locks and Hood River on the winding highway that clung precariously to the narrow strip of land between the towering cliffs and the broad river. Across the wide river to the north were the rolling hills that constituted the southern border of Washington State. In contrast to the Oregon side, these were gentle hills that contained farms and even a few vineyards. The hills were green in early June, though I knew from rainy experience they would probably still be green in September.

About half way through the journey along the gorge is the peculiarly named town The Dalles. It was about here that Alan and I seemed to exhaust the topic of Zen for a little while at least, and we continued east through the gorge in a comfortable silence. Gradually the forests and steep cliffs on the Oregon side gave way to more gently rolling hills, though the interstate still followed closely to the course of the river, not quite ready yet for the leap upward into the wheat fields of eastern Oregon. I was reminded, as I always was when reaching this part of the gorge, of the fields and farms in California's Central Valley, which I had driven through innumerable times as a child. I had realized long ago that I much preferred mountains and forests to fields and plains, but there nevertheless is a subtle and nuanced beauty in the grass and wheat, whether encountered in the green Oregon June or the golden California September.

Finally, almost two hundred miles east of Portland, the interstate rises suddenly out of the gorge and turns southeast across the expansive fields and farms, heading straight for the Blue Mountains in the distance. I spotted a Conoco station near Hermiston, and we got off the freeway to gas up the car and get a little snack. We sat for a few moments at the picnic table chained to the concrete alongside the little store, and soaked up a little sunshine while we ate our doughnuts. Finally Alan spoke.

"You certainly got quiet there for a while. Too much Zen for an early morning car ride?"

"Too much past. When you start wandering around on one path from way back when, it's hard not to find yourself looking down others."

"We agreed we'd only talk about stuff that can explain to me your puzzling new career in ministry, so I don't want to hear about paths that lead to all the girls you chased in your misspent youth."

"Ah, but there must be something deeply spiritual about chasing girls?"

"Well, in your case it would probably be a pretty short chase. So, c'mon; were you really thinking about girls that whole time?"

"Actually, I was thinking about forests and mountains. All of that stuff involving Zen happened in our home in Los Altos, but we had another home in the mountains where I spent all or part of every summer until I was in my thirties. Since I never practiced Zen, I would have to say that it is in those mountains that I had my first real, tangible experiences with the spiritual world."

"Cool!" Alan exclaimed. "Let's hit the road, and you can tell me all about it!"

We climbed back into the car and sped east towards Pendleton. I found myself again on another journey I had taken repeatedly as a child, and I wistfully wondered if there was any other metaphor that could be used for my life, but couldn't immediately come up with one. *Life on the road, I guess.* It seemed like an appropriate place to start, anyway.

"If you travel up Hwy. 108 for about thirty miles east out of Sonora in California's Gold Country, you'll see a turn off marked for Pinecrest Lake. Drive another mile down this road, and you will suddenly burst upon the shores of a blue-green jewel set in a bowl surrounded by pine and cedar forests and a backdrop of dramatic Sierra granite. In 1957, when I was 1 1/2

Part I: Themes

years old, my father rented a cabin on Pinecrest Lake for a two week vacation for himself and his young family. Thus began for me an association with Pinecrest that lasted thirty-two years, and a lifelong relationship with the sacred beauty and power of creation.

"Pinecrest Lake is a misnomer: it's actually a reservoir, which was constructed in 1914 to provide water for downstream communities and serve as a control dam for the hydroelectric plants located farther along the south fork of the Stanislaus River. Before being dammed, the river ran through a meadow that was used in the summer by the Miwok Indians, and was covered in several feet of snow during the winters. The road into the lake ends at the western shore: a sandy beach area that is the remnant of the glacial moraine, the effluvia left over from the glacier that carved through the surrounding granite to form the valley now filled with pent up water from the spring runoff. Looking out east from the beach you would see most of the small three hundred acre lake, and towering over the far shore the dominant feature of the area: a thousand foot wall of granite, sheared away by those ancient glaciers, looming over the lake. I don't know what this feature is officially called; we referred to it simply as Little Yosemite, and it's a powerful testament to the primal forces unleashed during earth's formation.

"The Forest Service allowed cabins to be built along the shores of the lake, and eventually a lodge and marina grew up at the end of the road on the western shore. A unique feature of the cabins built on the lake is that nearly all of them were (and still are) inaccessible by road. The only way to reach these cabins was either by boat or by hiking in along the lakeshore trail. The trail wound close to the lake, which was surrounded by forests of mixed conifers and the occasional aspen grove near the water, and interspersed on the steep hillsides with granite outcroppings. Cabins further east along the north and south shores were consequently quite isolated, a condition that was amplified in the winter when boating was not possible on the frozen lake and the lakeshore trail became treacherous. The Stanislaus river entered the lake at the east end, and a dusty trail ran along the south shore of the river, passing through a Boy Scout camp until it dumped out into a granite and scrub valley beneath Little Yosemite called—you guessed it—the Boy Scout valley.

"In 1957 Dad rented a place on the South Shore that was the last one reachable by road, then for the next two summers he rented a different cabin on the North Shore that was not reachable by road, which allowed him the excuse to purchase what he really wanted anyway: a brand new

Chapter 2: Nature

yellow speedboat with a Johnson outboard motor. Finally, in the fall of 1960, Dad purchased our cabin at 204 Lakeshore Trail. The cabin was just a few cabins down from the one owned by Win and Helen Wagener, who had introduced us to Pinecrest at about the same time they were introducing Mom to Zen. Now, instead of spending two week vacations at the lake, the entire summer was spent there. We would pack up and leave our home in Los Altos as soon as school let out in June and drive across California to the lake. These trips across the Central Valley were epic, and I particularly remember the fruit and vegetable stands along the dusty farm roads; but even more notable was the A&W root beer stand in Oakdale where we would always beg Mom and Dad to pleeeeeease stop. We would stay at the lake all summer until Labor Day and the beginning of school. Dad stayed in Los Altos during the week to work, and would drive up and stay with us at the cabin over the weekends.

"It would be a gross understatement to call these summers at Pinecrest idyllic. I spent three months of every year as a child wandering around in a mountain paradise, mostly unsupervised and unrestrained. I frequently had friends come up and stay a week or two and we spent most of our time sailing, swimming, hiking, and reading the paperbacks that Mom always brought along for our 'down' times. My Uncle Bill and Aunt Maggie were also frequent guests, along with their three daughters, my cousins. It was a place of family bonding just as if we were a normal middle class family. There was no television, and radio reception was iffy at best, so we spent hours playing Scrabble or Monopoly. The cabin had enough amenities to keep us comfortable—electricity, a phone, running water (usually) and indoor plumbing—but was isolated enough to keep us cut off from the outside world unless we actively sought it out by going over to the lodge."

"You were a privileged kid!" Alan exclaimed. "Not many people got that kind of experience."

"Yeah. I was privileged, though I didn't know it at the time. Most of my attention was focused on goofing off and having fun, yet I was aware even at an early age of a sacred presence around me. Today I would call Pinecrest a *thin place*, a phrase used in the Celtic tradition to describe those regions where God's presence is palpable. It's a place that exudes mystery and divinity, and I had experiences that underscored that sense every time we went to Pinecrest.

"Along with my brothers and sister, or with a friend, we would often take hikes from our cabin around to the east end of the lake and up into the

Part I: Themes

Boy Scout Valley. The trail in the valley scoots along the south bank of the river, which is dry and dusty, winding between gently sloping granite slabs. Along the north bank of the river, and visible from the trail, lies a green and lush meadow, dotted with aspen groves and teeming with birds, squirrels, and other wildlife. We were always separated from this meadow by the river, so my unrequited desire to walk those green pastures helped to magnify its mystery. I was convinced that it was the Garden of Eden and that God lived there. I have no idea how I even had heard of the Garden of Eden in my Zen/atheist home, but I could sense a sacred presence even if I couldn't really articulate it. Finally, as a teenager, my friend Jim and I managed to cross the river and enter the mysterious meadow. I assumed, as we waded across the depleted river, that I would be disappointed and would discover nothing more than a mountain meadow. But as we climbed the bank and crossed the meadow into one of its aspen groves, I was struck hard by the thought that God really did live here! The previously imagined sacred presence became real and palpable as we quietly listened to the quaking of the aspen leaves and smelled the fecund dampness of the meadow floor. The rotting carcasses of fallen trees provided ample sustenance for the grasses and flowers of the meadow, as well as cover for beavers, squirrels and a myriad of other wildlife. The mixture of sugar pines and aspens provided safe haven for hundreds of birds, who all squawked at the human intruders as we invaded their homes. Being boys, Jim and I eventually proceeded to our goal of ascending the steep hillside that rose out of the meadow, but I left there thoroughly convinced that God is present in God's own creation. And I have always felt blessed that one of my earliest mountaintop experiences came in a meadow, a daily reminder that God's presence is not exceptional: we are wrapped up in it.

"Of course this experience of the sacred was not limited to unusual times and places. At Pinecrest we were literally within nature twenty-four hours a day. Swimming in the cool waters of the lake meant squishing the sand between our fingers, diving deep into the waters of the little cove in front of our cabin, and letting the fish nibble at our toes as we dangled our feet from the dock. After swimming to the rocks that jutted out from the shore on the other side of the cove, we would climb up, scraping our knees, and let the warm breeze dry our bodies as we basked in the sunshine, splayed out on the rocks like ancient Sirens. Later in the day we might strap on our boots and take a hike up the steep hillside behind the cabin, moving away from the world of humans and into the realm of trees.

Chapter 2: Nature

"Forests have many occupants, both animal and plant, but they are clearly ruled by the trees. Up the slope behind our cabin grew huge conifers whose boughs controlled access to sunlight, and whose deep roots controlled all the moisture in their kingdom. Walking among these aristocrats you could feel life vibrating all around you. The trees moved, they had particular smells, and their gaze, usually of benign disinterest, followed you wherever you went."

Alan burst into my reverie, "It sounds like you were becoming a Druid!"

"Well, in a way. I wasn't conscious of it, of course, and I didn't know anything about the Druids until I was older. But I think even then I made an important distinction. The Druids believed that the trees were God, whereas I believed that God was in the trees. In other words, the trees had their own essence which participated with God, and God with them, but the trees were not God himself."

"Did you feel the same way about rocks and birds and grass?"

"Oh yes, and about myself too. And although there seems to be an affinity between living things which heightens the sense of God's presence in the forest kingdom, I think there is also an equality of that presence among all components of creation."

"Even bats? Volcanoes?"

"Yeah, even spiders and snakes. There were plenty of those at Pinecrest, and plenty of bats too, though no active volcanoes in the vicinity.

"About a hundred yards up the hill behind our cabin ran a rudimentary trail that provided access to the main water line. I can remember standing up there surrounded by trees, listening to the wind whisper through the boughs. At my feet ferns grew betwixt the rocks where water had seeped out of the old, wooden water line, and granite boulders, half buried in the dirt, patiently hosted families of lichen. On rare occasions a snake would be warming himself on one of these rocks where the sun was able to work through the canopy, and always there would be spider webs slung across the path, where unfortunate flies met their demise. In spots you could see through the trees to the lake far below, and the little dots of people in their boats or swimming seemed like they belonged to another world.

"I would hike down this scraggly little trail, following the water line, until I came upon a rocky spot where the trees had briefly abdicated their shroud in favor of the warm sun, and I would sit there in the quiet warmth and let my mind and body go. I was having a little mountain *zazen*, I guess. I wasn't really thinking about God. To paraphrase Paul, I was a child with

Part I: Themes

childish thoughts, and I suppose later as a teenager I was thinking about girls! But after a while, the noisy mind fades, and you simply experience the warm breeze on your cheek and the scratchy rock on your bottom without commentary. Time passes unnoticed, and the occasional undefined sound that wafts up the hill from the lake passes over you and around you, noticed but not retained. To tell you the truth, Alan, I've always struggled with most indoor forms of meditation. If I'm going to sit and be with God, I'd rather do it on a rock than on a cushion or a chair."

"Man!" Alan said. "Now that's what I'm talking about. No priests, no cathedrals, no rules, no books! Just me and nature." He looked pensive for a moment, then continued, "But you know, people fall off rocks, and they get bitten by snakes. How does that fit into your Druid idealism? How can you be intellectually honest if you romanticize the healing part of nature without regard to the hurting side of nature? Or in the lingo you're adopting, can you really say that God is only in the good things, and the bad things—the rabid bats and the devastating volcanoes—come from somewhere else?"

I smiled, recognizing the familiar and ancient argument. "No, all of creation comes from God, even the bats and volcanoes and spiders. But evil itself springs only out of human intent, the product of free will. I know I've hit on mostly the positive and no doubt romanticized spiritual moments in the mountains, but Pinecrest was also a great teacher of the dangers of creation. Danger can produce fear in a primal way, but it can also produce great clarity. There is no explicit or implicit promise made by God that the world God has created will be free of danger or fear. We might be killed at any moment by some natural process of creation, like a meteor striking us or a rabid bat flying into the car. But God is not a puppet-master who at the beginning of time placed all actions on a master script that is simply playing out inexorably now. How boring! There is no intent on God's part that a rabid bat fly into our car. In the large view of creation, bats—even rabid ones—serve a purpose in the evolution of all creation towards the peaceable kingdom of God, and it is for that purpose that bats were created. There is no 'plan' for an individual bat to bite you at a specific point in time, but there is a purpose that that bat participates in, just as you and I do."

Alan shook his head. "This is the clarity you found sitting on a rock in the forest?"

"Not exactly, though I do remember a moment of great clarity while sitting on another, much larger rock. You remember Little Yosemite, the giant rock edifice that towered a thousand feet above the east end of Pinecrest

Chapter 2: Nature

Lake? Well, you can get to the top of that cliff by hiking around to the back side—the north side—where there is a fairly gentle slope that leads to the top. One summer as a teenager Jim and I took the long hike around to the back side and up the slope until we finally made it to the top, where we rested by dangling our feet over the edge of the cliff. It was a fine, sunny day. To the east we could see far back into the high Sierra back country, with its mixture of solid granite and gentle forests. To the west lay the lake, with the little dots of sailboats floating gently across its blue-green waters. Below us was a sheer, thousand foot drop to the floor of the Boy Scout Valley, where we could still see the remains of shattered rock left behind when the glacier had ground through there thousands of years before. The warm breeze helped to cool us off, and after about half an hour, Jim, who sat at my left, got up and moved off to his left. I sat for a few more moments, then turned to my right, preparing to get up. That's when I heard the unmistakable sound of an upset rattlesnake less than a foot away."

"Ooh boy!"

"Yeah. In retrospect I realize that the cold-blooded rattler had been sunning himself just like I was and was probably too groggy to be of any real danger; but at the time I just froze. For a moment it passed through my mind that my only choices were to jump off a thousand foot cliff or get bitten by a rattlesnake. That snake and I stared at each other for what seemed like an eternity, though it was probably only a few seconds, then I leaped backwards away from the cliff and right over the snake while screaming to Jim, 'Snaaaaaaaaake!' We ran as fast as two terrified thirteen year olds could back down the hill."

Alan was unsuccessful at suppressing his laughter. "I wish I could have seen that!"

"It *is* a funny story now, but I'm telling you, there can be great clarity in moments like that. Of course, fear can just freeze your mind and shut you down, but sometimes it can make you hyper-aware, super-connected to everything around you. You're no longer external and analytical; you're right there in it, a part of it.[1] So when you do survive a scary, life-threatening situation, it connects you more thoroughly to creation, and by extension, God. So that incident didn't endear me to snakes, but I subsequently climbed up to the top of Little Yosemite many times after that, in part to

---

1. No one has described this sense of super-awareness in fear better than Gerald May in his story of the bear from *The Wisdom of Wilderness*.

help feel that clear connection. The only difference is I always checked the spot where I was sitting a little more thoroughly!"

"So, if a rabid bat flies into the car right now, you'll just appreciate creation more? You'd just be OK with that?"

"No. And I don't think God expects me to be *OK* with that. But I wouldn't blame it on God, and if I survived such an event I would have a choice of how to respond. I could either become neurotic from fear, and base all of my future actions on the possibility of another bat flying into my car and thus be controlled by that fear; or I could use the clarity that is the by-product of fear to understand my position in creation better, and yes, perhaps take reasonable precautions against bats, but let my life and faith be strengthened, not weakened, by such an experience."

"You could do that?"

"People do it every day."

"That's not what I asked."

I shook my head. "Not with the snake. But yeah, I've done it."

"Are you going to tell me about it?"

"Later. We're still at the beginning of the story, and that comes closer to the end."

With that we settled into a cryptic silence. The wheat fields of eastern Oregon were still going by, interspersed every now and then with grazing cattle and tiny towns that appeared to have three gas stations huddled around the freeway off-ramp, and little else. As the first hints of dusk appeared we began descending into the little valley that held the town of Pendleton. In all the years I had been making this drive, I never got to know any of the local eating establishments, but I knew the location of the Denny's by heart. We pulled off of the freeway and directly into the parking lot.

As we climbed out of the car, Alan said, "There's no bats in here, right?"

"Ha-ha. But maybe they have fresh rattlesnake on the menu."

Waitresses in these little towns always look tired, and their friendliness always seems to be begging you to take them away to somewhere, anywhere else. "Becky: Service with a Smile!" showed us to our table, and although I scoured the menu intently, I couldn't find any offering that included rattlesnake.

Chapter 3: Music

FOR ONCE ALAN WAS quiet as we munched on our chicken strips. You'd think that driving would be easy—you're just sitting on your butt all day—but it made all of my middle-aged joints ache, and we weren't even finished with the first of our three days. Still, there must be some secret ingredient in Pepsi and french fries, because after a few minutes of eating I could feel life returning.

"Sorry to keep boring you with all these memories," I said.

"What, are you kidding? So far as I can tell, by the age of ten you were a Zen-Druid. I don't know any other Zen-Druids. I kinda like this Zen-Druid kid, though it still doesn't help me at all understand how he became a Methodist—excuse me, a *United* Methodist minister."

"Well, I'm not one yet, not officially anyway. Still a week to go before ordination."

"Thinking of backing out?"

"Sometimes. I had such different aspirations for most of my life. In some ways I'm as puzzled as you are by how I ended up here."

Alan thought for a moment. "Was one of those aspirations music? Were you into music as a kid like you are now?"

I laughed. "Oh yes! Remember, I grew up in the sixties, and I really wanted to be a rock star. At first I wanted to be Paul McCartney, but later I decided on being a folk-rock star like Crosby, Stills and Nash."

"OK, OK! I sense another long story coming. I'll tell you what: let me get another cup of coffee to keep me awake, and maybe some pie, while you tell me all about becoming a Druid Crosby, Stills and Nash."

Part I: Themes

I laughed again. "Well, obviously I didn't quite make it, but I think it's fair to say that music has shaped my spirituality as much as my exposure to Zen and nature did."

I flagged down "Becky: Service with a Smile!" and ordered apple pie and coffee for both of us. As I gazed out the window I could see that, only a few weeks away from the longest day of the year, the sun was still loitering low on the horizon, poised to fall into the Pacific Ocean far away in the West in just a few minutes.

"Alright," Alan said, settling into his pie, "let's hear it."

"Well, growing up in the sixties in the San Francisco Bay Area, you really couldn't avoid rock music. The Jefferson Airplane hit it big when I was eleven years old, in 1967, followed by bands like the Grateful Dead and Quicksilver Messenger Service; these bands defined the San Francisco, Fillmore West kind of psychedelic rock music. I liked their music—to this day one of my goals in life is to be able to play *Embryonic Journey*[1]—but I wasn't into the psychedelic scene at all. For one thing, at twelve I was a little young, but I also found myself being drawn to a different style of music as I learned to play the guitar."

"How did that happen?"

"In that same year, 1967, my brother Charlie came down with the mumps and was confined at home for two weeks. Being bored to tears, he borrowed a guitar from a friend and, being a gifted natural musician, taught himself to play. Charlie is left-handed, so he played the guitar upside-down like Paul McCartney. He got pretty good pretty fast, and began entertaining us with Beatles songs and so forth. I couldn't stand that Charlie could do something that I couldn't so, using the same borrowed guitar, I started teaching myself as well. Thus began a lifelong, usually friendly, competition between brothers playing music. In all fairness, Charlie pretty much won this competition hands down. He not only had great natural ability, but he became an excellent student, learning to play and excel at the piano and the electric bass. I mostly just farted around on the guitar, but I had another musical outlet.

"In the fourth grade my parents rented me a cornet so that I could begin playing in the school band. Oh, how I loved that cornet! It's an instrument that has by now been almost totally supplanted by the trumpet, but the

---

1. *Embryonic Journey* is the classic and iconic solo guitar song by Jorma Kaukonen of the Jefferson Airplane, written in 1962 and released on the album *Surrealistic Pillow* in 1967.

cornet is one of the sweetest sounding brass instruments there is. Although I never really mastered the cornet either, playing in band broadened my musical horizons beyond the Beatles and San Francisco rock to the world of classical music. At about the same time my Dad bought a brand new stereo system and recordings of Broadway musicals, which he would play loudly while he lay on the sofa and pretended to conduct. In other words, by the time I was twelve my home was filled with an eclectic and wide range of musical styles, which led to my lifelong love of an eclectic and wide range of musical styles.

"In 1969 I became a teenager, and to be honest one of the big attractions of playing the guitar was that girls liked it. I had long red hair back then and walked around with a guitar strapped to my back, looking for all the world like a young hippie on the upswing. Thank God I wasn't into drugs, but I was certainly eager to attract a girlfriend. By 1971 my parents were able to buy me my first, and very cheap, acoustic guitar—which I still have—and I took it everywhere. Fortunately for me I found music that didn't require an electric guitar so, equipped with songs by Simon & Garfunkel, the Beatles and Crosby Stills and Nash, I set forth into the world of teenage girls. I was good enough to attract a crowd of listeners, but ironically it was my trumpet playing that snagged me my first girlfriend."

"I knew it!" Alan interjected. "I knew we'd get around to girls! Buddy, you're digressing. Unless your girlfriend was a teenage Zen master, please get back to how music led you to become a minister!"

"Well, sorry, but I guess like everybody my love life had something to do with my spiritual journey. Through playing the cornet, then later the trumpet, I got involved in my high school jazz band. It was a really good band, and we ended up playing at festivals around the Bay Area and appeared on a local TV show: that kind of thing. Julie, my high school girlfriend, was kind of a jazz band groupie who, amazingly, fixated on me. The band went to a competition in Monterey for a chance to play at the Monterey Jazz Festival, and Julie and her family came along, and, well, the rest is history. But, you know, that's how I viewed music back then. I liked it, but it was also the means to an end. There weren't any conscious connections with spirituality back then. I was in many ways a pretty unconscious kid, just absorbing music like I did Zen and nature in an unexamined way.

"And yet," said Alan sarcastically, "you said it was like, you know, super-important!"

"Did not!" We both laughed, then I continued.

Part I: Themes

"I'm trying to describe some of these formative experiences. I wasn't conscious of spirituality when I was around Suzuki-roshi either, I just felt it. I just absorbed it without analysis. The same is true of the natural world. I was in it, like a fish in water, but not necessarily consciously aware of it, as a fish is not aware of the water. But my entry into music, which later became instrumental—pun intended—to my spiritual development, was at the time rather venal. It elevated me socially and allowed me to compete with Charlie as the center of attention, and I acquired a pretty girlfriend because of it, but at the time I completely lacked the discipline to actually become a really good musician. But what I did absorb was the *possibility* of becoming a good musician, just as I absorbed from Suzuki-roshi and Pinecrest the possibility of becoming a Zen-Druid! And yes, I did then and at other times in my life aspire to become a professional musician, but that same lack of discipline always prevented me from doing so. At times, when I would really knuckle under and practice, I could get to be pretty good, but I just couldn't ever sustain it for very long.

"But I also became an excellent listener of music, which made up for my lack of performance abilities. In the early 1970s Seiji Ozawa was the conductor of the San Francisco Symphony, and he took that rather moribund institution and revitalized it. He brought the symphony down the peninsula to play concerts in the gym at Foothill Junior College in Los Altos. My mom, who loved all things Japanese, was delighted to take us all to see another Japanese phenom. Ozawa cut quite a figure on the podium, eschewing the traditional stiff white shirt and bow tie for a comfortable turtleneck underneath his tuxedo coat. But in spite of the absolutely abysmal acoustics of the college gym, the music was spectacular. At one concert he conducted the orchestra in Prokofiev's *Romeo and Juliet* and I was simply bowled over. But other performances of pieces by Beethoven and Tchaikovsky introduced me to the realm of absolute music."

"Absolute music?" Alan interjected.

"Music that doesn't have lyrics and is not programmatic: it's not trying to tell a particular story. Think of Bach's great *Toccata and Fugue in D Minor*: it's evocative, yes, but it isn't telling a story. Its meaning comes from within each listener. For some, the meaning is in the structure itself—the complexities of a fugue, for example—but others find the music to be evocative, stirring up emotions and associations that aren't tied to a particular narrative. But there's something else, something only the performers can provide; something mysterious that allows music to touch us beyond logic or analysis. Musicians know this; they talk about the difference between playing the notes and playing the music. Beginners are usually satisfied if they can just get all the notes correctly, but as a musician matures, if they desire to really elevate their game, they learn the notes quickly, then concentrate on interpretation. They try to meld their own uniqueness as a person with the intent of the composer expressed on the page to co-create the final performance. In other words, they try to blur the distinction between themselves and the music."

"Co-create? I thought the composer created the music, and the musicians just played it."

"Not exactly. Co-creation is a critical component of music that goes beyond the notes, and it is also critical to understanding our place in the relationship with God. That's why I'm telling you about this now, because out of music came for me what I call 'shared learnings.' Wisdom and knowledge acquired in one discipline become analogous and informative to another; in this case, the spiritual life. So, let me give you an example of co-creation and maybe you'll see the analogy.

"This happened much later when I was in college in Hayward and living in Berkeley. My friend Terry and I took BART into the City to hear the great classical guitarist Andrés Segovia. The train deposited us on Market St., and the concert was at a hall at the top of Nob Hill. We had counted on the cable cars to take us up California St., but they had already shut down for the night and we had to jog all the way up Nob Hill in order to arrive late to the concert. As we finally took our seats, still panting and sweating, Segovia was already on stage, all alone, of course. He sat in a little chair with his left foot up on the guitarist's foot rest. The man was pushing 80, and when he started to play it was clear that his technique was starting to fade. I don't know if I've ever heard so many flubbed notes outside of a junior high school band concert. But I didn't care, and neither did anyone else in the audience, because he could overcome the limitations of his technique by playing the music beautifully. It was an extraordinary experience. He owned the guitar from bridge to nut, and it willingly forgave his aging fingers in order to produce great beauty for the master. The distinctions between himself, the instrument and the music became blurred. Bach, Vivaldi and Telemann may have provided the notes, but Segovia provided the soul."

"Well, this certainly sounds spiritual: souls and co-creating?"

"Absolutely. I ultimately discovered in those concerts in that horrible gym at Foothill, and in concerts like the one Segovia gave, that there is a

37

very spiritual place in music, and that there is a very musical place in the spirit, for me. They are not simply analogous; they are also connected."

The apple pies and coffee had disappeared, and although "Becky: Service with a Smile!" had been loitering around tentatively, she finally wearied of our conversation and boldly approached the table with the bill in hand.

"I got it," I said, and placed my credit card in the little folder. When she returned with the slip, I gave her a generous tip for her patience, but I noticed that look of yearning to get away had returned to her tired face, and Alan and I got up quickly and returned to the car.

Chapter 4: Christianity

As we drove out of the valley into the thickening gloom of night, Alan asked, "Say, wasn't this about the time that Christian pop music hit the scene? Since you were so into music, did you get into that at all?"

"There was some Christian rock around in the early '70s, but it was for . . . well, Christians, so I was oblivious. And when Christian praise music started up in the early '80s it seemed very fundamentalist and not terrifically good musically—and I wasn't a Christian—so no, I wasn't into that scene at all. In spite of all that, I nevertheless did get my first meaningful introduction to Christianity through a couple of pop culture phenomena."

"I thought you said Christianity was pretty much a non-presence in your life when you were growing up."

"Well, I did, but I guess that's not entirely accurate. In the sixties and seventies, Christianity was still part of the basic fabric of American society. References to the Bible, Jesus and God were made consistently even in otherwise secular contexts. The fact that a band called the *Doobie Brothers* could have a hit in 1972, ten years before the beginnings of Christian praise music, called *Jesus is Just Alright With Me* speaks for itself. But all of these popular culture references to Christianity didn't form a particularly solid basis for any kind of understanding of the faith. I never opened the Bible, never heard a sermon, and never had any substantive talks about Christianity until I was in my twenties.

"Ironically, there was a Methodist church just around the corner from our home in Los Altos. Its main attraction to me as a kid was that they had installed speed bumps in the lanes leading to their parking lot, and I spent many hours using them like ski jumps on my skateboard and bicycle. There also was a little creek that ran behind the church, and a few times my buddy Mark Galen and I would sneak down there and try to smoke cigarettes that I had liberated from my mom. I was never able to inhale without hacking, coughing and turning green, so this ultimately was a great lesson in teaching me how hideous smoking is; but hanging out with Mark was the main goal. Mark was the designated 'bad boy' of our neighborhood, and he was constantly in trouble at home and at school. For all I know he might be a bank president now, but back then his penchant for juvenile delinquency made him fun and attractive. He also gave me my first formal introduction to fundamentalist Christianity.

"Mark's mother was quite devout, and she was concerned that I wasn't 'saved.' One afternoon when I was about 11, Mark invited me to come to his church (Baptist, I think, but it certainly wasn't the Methodist church) and meet with him and his mother. We gathered in a windowless room in the back of the church, where Mark's mother instructed me to close my eyes and pray for Jesus to enter my heart. And I did. I so wanted Jesus to enter my heart, and I prayed fervently that Jesus would do so. The truth was, I didn't have any feeling of belonging to my mom's Zen group, or really any other group, but if Jesus would just enter my heart I might belong to that group. I wasn't really sure what that group specifically was, but I really wanted to belong. I was overwhelmed by the emotional, cathartic feeling that this kind of experience can bring, and I cried and told Mrs. Galen that Jesus had indeed entered my heart. But . . . that was the end of it. After the emotionalism ebbed, I could detect no evidence at all that Jesus had entered my heart, and even at that young age I suspected it had all been a setup. I'm sure Mrs. Galen's motives were good, but the net result was reinforcement of the idea that Christianity was phony. When I didn't join their church or participate at all, Mark and I gradually grew apart, and he went out of my life before we were out of elementary school.

"If God was trying a direct approach on me, it wasn't working, but I realize now God's indirect efforts were having spectacular results. For example, during the mid-sixties my father was frequently away from home on business trips, and instead of eating our dinners at the formal dining room table, Mom would serve a casual meal to us in the kitchen, and read aloud to us from the works of J.R.R. Tolkien. We started with *The Hobbit* and over the course of a few years made our way through *The Lord of The Rings* in its entirety. Considering the length of *The Lord of The Rings*, looking back I am not only impressed with my mother's perseverance, but also with the

Chapter 4: Christianity

frequency and duration of Dad's business trips. I did not know back then that Tolkien was a devout Catholic, but the clear exposition of heroic Christian values made an indelible impression on me."

"So, basically, you didn't learn Christian values from the Bible or church, you learned them from Frodo?"

I laughed. "That would be about right. Of course, Christian values in some form or another permeated American society whether you were conscious of it or not. They were, and are, the basis for the construction of our society not just for Christians, but for American Jews, Muslims, Buddhists; even atheists. But *The Lord of The Rings* is so skillfully written to draw you into those values, to clearly explicate how important they are, and to draw very clear lines between not only Good and Evil, but also between values that lead to good and values that lead to evil. For example, the seduction of Saruman from being the White Wizard and head of the wizard's council, to being a hapless lackey of Sauron, is a clear and compelling moral lesson on the pitfalls of power that spoke to me back then much more powerfully than the stories of Herod and Pilate.

"But the most compelling narrative in *The Lord of The Rings* is that of serving a cause greater than yourself. Frodo has all sorts of options to avoid his fate, or to pass the burden of the ring on to others, but he does not take them. And in a very human-like—or at least Hobbit-like—fashion, he has doubt, dismay and betrayal on his path: it's not easy, not at all. But at the core of every Hobbit is a rock-solid belief in the Good, which at times must be defended at all costs, including your own life. Isn't this precisely the message of Jesus' life? Aren't all of us called to serve the greater Good, whether we name it God or not? I am thankful that I have not had to put my own life on the line or been tested like Frodo was, but this value of serving something greater than yourself was a timely fit with the idealism, if not the reality, of the sixties. The connection that was missing for me was with the idealism of hope that is inherent in Christianity. I never heard that part.

"*The Lord of The Rings* portrays these values in a romantic light. Not romantic in the sense we often use it now, meaning love and sex, of which there is hardly any in these books; but in the older sense of heightened feelings and awareness that lead to noble actions. All of the characters on the good side—Frodo, Sam, Gandalf, Aragorn etc.—don't act on tactics or strategy designed to create advantage for themselves personally. Instead, there is an inherent nobility in each of them, out of which springs their actions, often without any clear tactical direction. This too is a core Christian message, that each of us is given an Image of God, an inherent part of our beings, out of which spring the actions of our own lives, even when those actions require great faith. Evil arises from those who corrode this Image, who are seduced by power like Saruman or who fall prey to cynicism and fear, like the Steward of Gondor, Denethor. In the books this corrosion of the Image of God leads to the ultimate destruction of these characters, something that sadly is not always true in the real world; but nevertheless their stories expressed to me a powerful message about the necessity of listening to the still, small voice of faith even in the darkest corners of our lives, if for no other reason than to combat the corrosion of your own Image of God.

"And finally Tolkien explores the bittersweet nature of this world, and how it is a painful necessity in life. You might recall that Frodo, after fulfilling his mission, tries to return to his former life as a quiet Hobbit of the Shire, but he can't. He's seen too much, done too much, and has truly been changed—transformed—by his experience. He can only find ultimate peace by sailing into the West—the Nordic heaven in Tolkien's mythology—with Gandalf and Bilbo. The immortal Elves, like Elrond and Galadriel, must also leave Middle-Earth with sadness and loss, even though they were fully aware they were returning to a glistening heaven. And of course, there's Arwen. If you were a dedicated reader and went through the appendices of *The Lord of The Rings*, you discovered that Arwen, Elrond's daughter who became mortal in order to wed Aragorn, is finally left alone and sobbing in the abandoned forests of Lothlorién after Aragorn's death. She is filled with sorrow, but not regret. Bittersweet.

"Perhaps some people would not consider this bittersweetness a Christian aesthetic, but we forget that Jesus himself suffered loss and its consequent emotions at the death of Lazarus and the forecast of Jerusalem's demise. God gave us a world we can love, and even if we are conscious of the world as God's gift to us we are so intertwined with it that we must bid farewell reluctantly. Transformation inevitably involves loss. God doesn't want us to die, God wants us to live, a counterpoint that Tolkien captures perfectly through the lives of his characters, both mortal and immortal."

"So, wow, you're pretty passionate about this. Why weren't you converted on the spot?"

"Because I wasn't hearing this from a Christian source! I had no idea these were Christian values. The Christianity I was conscious of from the culture around me seemed to have a focus on salvation and life after death,

Chapter 4: Christianity

with a strong undercurrent of the sinfulness of humanity. It seemed rule based and cold, and it simply could not hold my attention like the exciting adventures of the Hobbits. Why do you think Tolkien's books were so popular? Hidden within the adventure was a story about the nobility of humanity, the necessity of faith, and the power of the two when combined to overcome evil. And it was, of course, a powerful story of a journey. All of these ideals still resonated with large segments of the population; ideals that were originally transmitted through the Christian religion. But Christianity as it was practiced in suburban America in the 1960s seemed almost totally at odds with these ideals."

"OK, so, wow, you're pretty passionate about this, too. Why did you convert at all?"

"Because I was ultimately wrong. Behind the church's stoic and monolithic walls was a hidden church and a true Christ; the real Christ whose aesthetic Tolkien had captured so well in fiction, but the church had obscured over the years in its zeal for conformity and orthodoxy. The full realization of this has only come recently in my life, but I read and reread *The Lord of The Rings* over and over through the years, a clear sign that I was seeking in Tolkien's fiction what I later would find in the Gospels."

Alan remained silent for a while, chewing over our philosophical discussion, I guess. The sun had set behind us in the west as we started up the steep incline east of Pendleton into the Blue Mountains of eastern Oregon. Baker was still an hour or so away, and I began to wonder if we would finish the first leg of our trip in silence. But finally, Alan spoke again.

"I just find it hard to believe that there was nothing in your childhood to connect you to Christianity. Most people don't become convinced of something later in life if there wasn't a seed planted early on. There must have been something positive about religion in your early life? Didn't you say that *Superstar* had a big influence on you?"

"Religion, or at least Christianity, didn't really connect for me. But yes, through *Jesus Christ, Superstar* I began a sort of connection with Christ himself. You recall how I said that fully Christian statements, like 'Jesus is Just Alright With Me' were completely acceptable in popular culture, and by artists who were simultaneously producing secular music? So when the rock opera *Jesus Christ Superstar* was released in 1971, it became a smash hit, not only for its use of rock music and rock musicians in a story-telling format, but for its distinctly humanist take on the Passion story of Jesus. And passionate it was! I couldn't believe that they would engage Ian Gillan,

43

a well-known 'screamer' from the rock band Deep Purple, to portray Jesus. The story line diverged significantly from the Gospels in terms of the relationships between Jesus, Judas and Mary Magdalene in order to increase the drama and the passion, but since I didn't know the Gospels my enjoyment was unfettered by such details. Yes, yes, I know: *Jesus Christ, Superstar* might seem to some like a crappy introduction to Christianity, but for me at that time both in my life and in the world around me, it was perfect.

"Jesus wasn't cold, or distant, or stoic, or monolithic. Jesus had a passionate relationship with God." Much to Alan's annoyance, I started to sing loudly from *Superstar*.

"Please don't do that," he said, getting annoyed.

"Why not? This stuff was awesome to a fifteen year old agnostic!" I sang a little more, then remarked, "Every Christian ever born has at one time or another wondered if they knew how to love Jesus."

"C'mon man, keep it down. You almost had me lulled to sleep there with the Hobbits!"

"Oh, boo-hoo. I think I can say without reservation that if I had never heard *Jesus Christ, Superstar* I would never have become a Christian."

"But one of the enduring criticisms of *Superstar* is that it stops at Jesus' death, and doesn't include the resurrection."

"And so it should come as no surprise that I am primarily an incarnationalist."

"A what?"

"Incarnationalist. I connect more with Christ through his birth than through his death and resurrection. Remind me later and I can dig up a quote for you about that from a modern mystic, but for me, well, I'm a human, and while I believe in the divine/human amalgamation that is Jesus Christ, it's difficult to relate personally to Jesus the Divine. This is exactly what Lloyd-Weber and Tim Rice were going for in *Superstar*. They took the most famous person in history, Jesus Christ, and his most dramatic story, the Passion, and milked it for all it was worth in terms of human emotion. A deep exegesis of Jesus and the meaning of the Gospels? Hardly. But it was pivotal for me, and I expect for others as well, in delivering Jesus out of the frigid confines of doctrine and catechism into a place where I could connect the dots between me, Jesus, and God. And just like I read Tolkien over and over again, I listened to that album over and over again. Probably a little OCD, I guess, but I realize now I was grasping for something that was just beyond my reach."

Chapter 4: Christianity

We had powered our way up the steep incline and come out into the Blue Mountains, bobbing up and down through the mountainous ridges and valleys until we reached La Grande. From there a long sloping valley led us south until we finally passed a sign that said "Baker City 1.5 miles," next to a billboard with an advertisement for our motel. It was completely dark, and the lights of the town of Baker itself were some distance off to the west of the freeway, so I stopped talking and concentrated on finding the exit. The Motel 8 stood out like a beacon amidst the sparse farmlands that were bisected by the freeway, and we pulled into the covered entryway and parked under the sign that promised a "Free Continental Breakfast!" I looked over at Alan, who finally said, "That's a hell of a story. You haven't stopped talking since Gresham, and I'm exhausted."

"Well, tomorrow's another long day, and we're only up to about 1971." I got out of the car and went over to the passenger side to help Alan out and guide him into the registration area. "I guess tomorrow we'll start with that phase of my life where the poop really hit the fan."

I'm not completely sure, but I think I heard my agnostic friend Alan mutter to himself as he rambled into the motel, "O dear God, there's more..."

Part II: Dissonance

The more obstinately you try to learn how to shoot the arrow for the sake of hitting the goal, the less you will succeed in the one and the further the other will recede.

—EUGEN HERRIGEL, *ZEN IN THE ART OF ARCHERY*

Chapter 5: Family & Zen

EVEN IN JUNE THE nights cool off significantly in the mountains of eastern Oregon, creating chilly, frosty mornings. I regretted not putting on my coat as I dragged my suitcase back out to the car. The frost lay lightly on the hay fields around the motel, and the sun made its presence known by the ambient light that spilled over the mountain ridges. The stillness was broken only by the impatient rustle of early morning cars going by on the nearby freeway. I tossed my bag into the trunk and went back into the motel for my "Free Continental Breakfast!" Alan was already there, having availed himself of some stale toast and cold bacon to accompany the acidic coffee. Hey, it was all free.

"You about ready to go?"

Alan turned slightly towards me and grunted. "Mother of God! Please allow a little more time for this coffee to burn away my stomach lining."

"Well, I see you're pretty grumpy this morning."

"If you like this, just wait until this afternoon."

After a few minutes I was finally able to tear Alan away from his gourmet breakfast, and while carrying his bags in one hand, and a greasy blueberry muffin in the other, I guided him out into the parking lot and settled him into the passenger seat of the car. With our bags stowed away I climbed in behind the wheel, balanced the muffin next to the shift lever, and started the engine.

"Where are we going today?"

"We're going to try and make it to Evanston."

"No, no, that's not what I meant. We spent all day yesterday—all 10 friggin' hours—exploring your idyllic childhood and your development

Part II: Dissonance

into a musical Zen-Druid. You hinted we might get into some crap today, so I figure the earlier we start, the sooner I'll be able to take a nap."

"Nice—real nice." I stopped at the adjoining gas station and filled the tank, then got back in and guided the car back up onto the freeway. "Do you want to hear this or not?"

"Well, there's no radio out here and this cheap rental doesn't have Sirius XM so, yeah. Go ahead and tell me how all of the nicely constructed nothingness of your childhood which you were completely unconscious of turned into crap as a teenager."

"Well, it didn't all turn to crap and it didn't all happen at once, but you're basically right. The main themes we talked about from my childhood—Zen, nature, music and religion—were still largely unexamined as I graduated from high school in 1973. I chose to continue living at home and attended college at Foothill Junior College, which was just a mile away. I commuted there on my Vespa scooter, and later on an actual real motorcycle. It was around this time that the most corrosive element of my life began to become so obvious that I could no longer ignore it. My Dad's boozing was getting out of control. Actually, it had been out of control for years but had remained mostly out of my sight, and certainly was never discussed. But by the early 1970s, if Dad wasn't at work he was drinking, and I suspect he may have been drinking at work, too.

"Even at the age of seventeen, I knew my parents' marriage was crumbling under the weight of severe dysfunction. Mom continued to go to Pinecrest and spend the summers there because, as she told me flat out, 'I need to get away from *him*.' In those days, as far as I was concerned, Mom could do no wrong just as Dad could do no right, and it wasn't until later that I realized she had enabled his alcoholism in a variety of ways. Unconsciously, I took it upon myself to become the anti-enabler and pathetically tried to save my parents' marriage by trying to stop Dad's alcoholism. I was quickly becoming the poster child for adult children of alcoholic parents and developed all of the associated neuroses.

"Thus began a long period in my life in which I felt that most of my endeavors failed and that life consisted of a long stream of dreary emotional dramas. I used to not describe this period to anyone in great detail because I felt so ashamed of it. I refer to it as my 'loser' period. This is of course a classic symptom of a child of alcoholic parents in which everything was my fault and it was up to me, worthless as I was, to fix everything. I guess we'd like to think that our spiritual journey moves forward only on high

Chapter 5: Family & Zen

mountain tops or in pleasant meadows, but I have learned that a great deal of travel takes place in the spiritual deserts of our lives. We seem incapable of truly knowing joy unless we have experienced deep pain."

We had reached the end of the valley where the freeway drops off into a freefall tumble all the way to the Idaho border. The surrounding hills were sandy and dotted with scrub, so it was no surprise to pass the collapsing ruins of a gigantic cement factory. It looked like the set of some apocalyptic Schwarzenegger movie. I though how apocalypse seemed like an appropriate image right now.

"Most years as I was growing up there would be an annual trip to Pinecrest in May in order to open up the place for the summer. These were called 'stag parties' and Dad would invite friends from work to come up there for an all-male weekend of poker and drinking, interspersed with work around the cabin. I have no idea what possessed my Dad to think it was appropriate for a teenage boy to come along for these weekends, but I nevertheless was taken along; probably to fix the plumbing under the toilet! Since Pinecrest was a reservoir the water was drained out considerably for the winter, and by May was not yet filled all the way back up. One Memorial Day weekend we were at the cabin for a stag party, and Dad wandered down to the beach in front of the cabin with a bottle of scotch, which he managed to empty. At about 10 a.m. we heard some yelling from the beach, and went and stood at the edge of the porch to see what the fuss was about. Dad had tied the shoelaces of his boots to each other, so that when he shakily stood up and tried to walk, he tripped and fell flat on his face. After a couple of meager attempts he simply sat on the beach complaining, unable to fathom the source of his problem. It retrospect this seems almost comical, but believe me, at the time it contained no humor whatsoever. I was deeply humiliated, and Dad's friends were shocked and embarrassed as they went down there to untie his shoes and escort him back up the hill to the cabin. It was at that moment that I lost Dad forever."

"Jesus. I'm sorry. I had no idea."

"Well, nobody really does, because I rarely talk about it. By my second year of college I was the only kid left at home. Norm and Hattie Lou had left years ago to go to college and to get on with their own lives, and in September of 1974 Charlie had departed for Boston to attend the Berklee School of Music. If such a thing were possible, the house in Los Altos had grown even more tense. I tried to convince my parents that the house was too big for them now that it was just the three of us, and I even managed to

Part II: Dissonance

get them to look at some other homes in the hopes this might restart their marriage, but nothing came of it. Then one day in April of 1975, when Dad was away on a business trip, Mom calmly announced to me that she would be leaving Dad that day and going to stay with a friend. I wasn't surprised, but after we talked I realized it was going to be just Dad and me at home. That evening I was up in Marin County playing a gig with a little combo at a party, and didn't arrive home until nearly midnight. Dad had gotten home from the airport before me, but was nowhere to be found. There I was, all of nineteen years old, going through each room in the house convinced that Dad had killed himself and I would discover his choked and bloody body. But after a thorough if reluctant search, including a suspicious examination of the swimming pool, I realized that he simply wasn't there. I went back into the kitchen, and it was then that I saw the phone book opened up on the kitchen table to the page for taxis. Mom had taken one car and I the other, so Dad was stuck without transportation when he got home. Ever the creative alcoholic, he had managed to come up with the means to run away from his problems. Completely disgusted, I went to bed.

"When I woke up late the next morning, Dad was in the kitchen fixing some coffee. I asked him where he had gone last night, and he sheepishly replied, 'To a bar.' For the next two months those were essentially the last words we spoke to each other. I would come home from school, or anywhere else I could be to stay out of the house, and Dad would fix chicken pot pies for us to have for dinner. We would sit at the table in complete and very tense silence while we ate, then I would get up and disappear into my room. To this day I will absolutely *not* eat a chicken pot pie.

"When summer finally came around Charlie came home from Boston to ease the tension somewhat, but Dad decided to put the house in Los Altos up for sale. It had not been maintained very well—Dad never really maintained anything—so it sold at a low price to people who were going to flip it. By mid-July I no longer had a place to live. Dad had an apartment in San Carlos, Mom was renting a room in Ladera, and I wound up sponging off of some of Charlie's friends who had rented a house for the summer in Los Altos Hills. The worst part of all this was that not only had my parents abandoned me, but they placed on me the responsibility for taking care of our two dogs. We had acquired a female Australian Shepherd named Honey B many years before, and had recently added a young male named Hannibal. Because Hannibal was young enough I was able to give him back to the couple we had bought him from at their ranch near Pinecrest, but

Chapter 5: Family & Zen

Honey B had to be euthanized: she was too old and irascible to be placed anywhere. The vet performed the procedure on the front lawn of the house where I was staying in Los Altos Hills, and after he carried her body away I remember returning to the house and crying my eyes out until all I could see was blackness. Had Vivian been around then she might have called this a black night of the soul; to me, it was a black pit of existence, starved of light and life. But of course, eventually my sight returned and I went on with life. For better or worse, I had learned the lessons of denial very well from my parents, and in the fall I moved across the bay to begin college at Cal. State, Hayward. Nevertheless, it was many, many years before I could forgive my parents for that summer and for pushing me into that black pit."

"Parents are crappy, and I hate it when it involves pets. Were your parents just thoughtless or cruel?"

"Yes." I didn't really want to dwell there, so I quickly moved on.

"It is probably not a coincidence that in the years when my parents' marriage was falling apart, things were also falling apart for my Mom's involvement with Zen. Things were just falling apart for her. In 1970, Suzuki-roshi anointed Richard Baker to be his successor both as abbot of the San Francisco Zen Center and as his spiritual successor through the Zen tradition of *dharma-transmittal*. I remember my mom saying at the time she thought he was the wrong man for this. He was the only person to receive dharma-transmittal from Shunryu Suzuki, which perhaps highlighted a blind side in the great teacher's judgment of the American adoption of Zen. After Suzuki-roshi died in 1971, San Francisco Zen Center plunged into a decade of scandal and chaos,[1] and the little Los Altos *zendo* began trying to distance itself from the Zen Center, which led to even more chaos and confusion. There certainly seemed to be cultural collisions going on between the Japanese *senseis* left in Suzuki's wake and the Americans taking over Zen Center.

"What Mom finally realized is that Zen Buddhism held no special magic when it came to relationships or moral behavior. She had abandoned Christianity because of its perceived hypocrisy and lack of a contemplative path, but eventually lost patience with Zen because of its lack of social consciousness and inability to reconcile eastern and western values which, she believed, led to a lack of moral restraint in some of its leaders. With all the drama and pain in her personal life, she did not want to participate in

---

1. For more information about the scandals at Zen Center in the 1970s, read Michael Downing's *Shoes Outside the Door: Desire, Devotion, and Excess at San Francisco Zen Center*.

Part II: Dissonance

this Buddhist drama and pain, and so backed away from the little Los Altos *zendo*. I'm pretty sure the last straw came as the rumors about Richard Baker's sexual excesses with young female Zen students began to surface. In fact, Baker was eventually removed as the Abbot of Zen Center after he had an affair with the wife of one of the Center's main benefactors. The scandals hit awfully close to home for my mom, and her reaction—pulling away from Zen—only served to confirm for me the untrustworthiness of religious leaders. The whole thing just fed into my growing distrust for organized religion, particularly because it hurt people I loved, like my mom. So, by the time I left home in the fall of 1975 to go to college, my family had almost no contact with the Bay Area Zen community.

"This whole experience was distasteful to say the least, but it was also my first experience with the kind of bipolar behavior organized religious institutions can demonstrate. It's a Dr. Jekyll and Mr. Hyde sort of thing. On the one hand you have the deeply spiritual and highly dedicated leader, like Suzuki-roshi, who guides his flock along the spiritual path with great care and integrity, but who is all too often followed by leaders with less depth who either fumble the whole thing or who bring into the temple some personal agenda that only serves to alienate and divide.

"Because the Zen community was wrapped up in my mind with my parents' personal problems, and in the absence of the integrity of a roshi like Shunryu Suzuki, I loosed my already tenuous grip on Zen and hung out the *Vacant* sign at my religious motel. I still resonated with the aesthetic that Zen Buddhism generated, but could find no way to personally connect with that aesthetic without the personal presence of Suzuki-roshi. Ironically, this was a time in my life when I was beginning to rail against the dangers of charismatic Christian leaders, conveniently forgetting that it was Suzuki-roshi's Zen charisma that had laid the foundations of my own spiritual development. Nevertheless, as I entered my junior year in college I was completely soured on religion, conventional or spiritual, Buddhist or Christian. With my parents separated and my siblings scattered, I felt as if I had no family at all. I turned my attention to studying music and enjoying college life, for the first time living away from home."

"Your religious motel? Really?" Alan shook his head. "But I think you're lying again. If you had so completely turned your back on Zen then we wouldn't be talking about it now. Just like *Jesus Christ Superstar* kept your interest in Christ alive, I suspect something kept your interest in Zen alive too. What was it?"

Chapter 5: Family & Zen

I thought for a moment and once again took in my surroundings. The sandy hills had given way to a flatter road winding along the Snake River. As the river headed north we headed south, eventually passing into the Mountain Time zone, even while we were still on the Oregon side. The irony of being on a long road trip while explaining the book that had kept Zen alive for me was about to become apparent.

"I guess you're right. I can get so focused on the crap that I forget there were some good things during those days. And, just as with *Superstar*, it turned out to be another pop culture phenomenon that redeemed Zen for me. In 1975, Robert Pirsig published the paperback version of his classic tale *Zen and the Art of Motorcycle Maintenance*."

"You're kidding, right? Is that an actual book?"

"It is, you illiterate, and despite its unusual title it is a fascinating and compelling book. The title is actually a spoof on the title of the most famous book about Zen in the west, *Zen in The Art of Archery*, but Pirsig makes it clear that the book should not be confused with the great body of texts on orthodox Zen, and that it isn't particularly valuable in terms of motorcycle maintenance either."

"Ha-ha-ha. So what is it about?"

"Pirsig was a rhetorician, and spends a lot of the book parsing the meaning out of phrases and actions that people say or do. But he wraps this story around his personal journey through madness and paints it all on the canvas of a motorcycle journey he takes with his son, Christopher, from Minnesota to San Francisco."

"Sort of like a car trip from Portland to Denver?" Alan asked dryly.

"Well, yeah, something like that. Anyway, a lot of it, as you might guess, comes from his love of rhetoric which translates into the importance of the precise meaning of words. But he makes some important comments about Zen that helped me immensely to connect with Zen on my own, instead of through my mother.

"He manages to get across the simple concept that Zen isn't just sitting, Zen isn't navel gazing: Zen is how you live. As the book swirls around the rhetorical meaning of 'quality,' it becomes clear that Zen, for Pirsig, is also about quality. If you want an outcome to turn out well, say for example, repairing a motorcycle, you need to do the task well. Yet 'quality' isn't simply a measure of the outcome, it is a measure of how well you perform each component of the task. He is applying to motorcycle repair what Herrigel applied to archery in *Zen in the Art of Archery*. You are a good archer when you perform the act of archery perfectly, in harmony with the bow, the arrow and yourself. Hitting the target is the result, not the goal. If the motorcycle you're working on is a metaphor for yourself, the same is true. Zen is the attempt to bring a person to attentiveness to all aspects of their existence, and to be aware of their total connectedness with everything around them."

I thought about that for a moment, then added for emphasis, "Zen is the art of cultivating awareness. Of seeing truly. Like the super-awareness that can come from fear, but deliberately practiced. Enlightenment is the result, not the goal."

Alan, in an attempt to keep the tires on the ground, said, "That doesn't sound very Methodist to me."

"That's because you don't know anything about Methodism. In the 1970s I didn't know anything about Methodism either. The idea of wholeness and completeness and super-awareness through the spiritual life seemed the sole purview of Zen Buddhism, and even that seemed more of an ideal than an achievable reality. Mom was disillusioned, Zen now had clay feet, and I was spinning in a void. I grasped onto music for dear life, hoping that somewhere in that vast field I would find the meaning that Zen promised, but was not delivering."

We finally reached the little town of Ontario, Oregon, where we crossed the Snake River and drove into Idaho. A few miles in we found a gas station with a little grocery store where we filled up the car and bought our daily dose of junk food for our mid-morning snack. In a matter of minutes we were speeding towards Boise through the rolling farmlands of western Idaho, and I jumped right back into my story.

Chapter 6: Art & Authenticity

"I entered Foothill Junior College in the fall of 1973 as a music major. I still had a very idealistic view of music, as well as a belief that I could succeed as a musician. That belief was not well founded, since I was now surrounded by ambitious people who practiced constantly in order to master their craft. I simply was unable to discipline myself that way, and found myself holding down the fifth trumpet chair and envying my colleagues, including my gifted brother Charlie who had preceded me at college and had proven himself valuable as a jazz bass player. However, my time at Foothill was not a complete waste, as I discovered that while I was pretty limited as a performer, I could explore musical ideas more successfully as a composer, and changed my focus to that discipline.

"One of the great challenges in music, both performing and composing, is finding a voice that is authentically your own. It's easy to be derivative and imitative, and it is in that mode that all beginners start out as they study what others have done. But eventually you need to have something of your own to contribute or you'll never be anything more than a dilettante. Occasionally an artist will come along and have commercial success by cleverly combining existing forms that give the appearance of being something new; the music may be familiar and accessible, but to me it ultimately lacks the heart to truly inspire. During my time at Foothill one such artist, or so I thought, was Chuck Mangione, and because of my skepticism I was a little apprehensive when he visited our school to do a workshop.

"Mangione at that time was riding the wave of success from his recordings of a sort of orchestrated jazz mixed with pop that produced such hits as *The Land of Make Believe*. Mangione also played the flugelhorn on

Part II: Dissonance

these recordings, which helped popularize this previously obscure instrument. The flugelhorn is a mellower version of the trumpet, and in 1974 mellow was beginning to replace the raw rock 'n roll of the sixties. Having grown up on raw, I had a hard time taking mellow seriously. I felt for all of his commercial success, Mangione's music lacked the authenticity of a great artist. It sounded forced, like he was trying too hard. So I attended his seminar with a lot of skepticism.

"Mangione talked a while about the music business and some of his experiences, but when someone asked him how he'd gotten his start, he lit up. It turned out he was an old be-bop jazz player, and he and his combo did a little set for us right there in the Foothill music room. Be-bop is, as the name implies, jumpy and highly improvisational, not anything like the over-orchestrated hits Mangione had produced, and it was obvious that this was where his heart was. The funny thing was, he was only an adequate player and would never be able to put himself beside some of the great be-bop artists like Charlie Parker or Dizzy Gillespie. Nevertheless, I found the average but more authentic be-bop Mangione much preferable to the successful but over-orchestrated Mangione. I'm pretty sure I'm letting some kind of musical snobbery slip out here—Mangione has had a very successful career—but this may also be a factor in my own inability to have a successful music career. Authenticity and success don't always go hand-in-hand, and you still have to be pretty good to get both. Practice is the key.

"I also made the mistake at this time in believing that some of my deficiencies as a musician might be corrected if I went the university route for training, so after two years at Foothill JC, I moved across the bay to attend California State University at Hayward. The truth I did not realize then is that universities produce theorists, not musicians. University music departments have to compete for grants just like the science and math departments, so it is helpful to create 'provable' music: music you can justify in a grant proposal without regard to its creativity or depth of meaning. The fact that I was not a good musician but was pretty good at theory simply reinforced the false value of the university education, as I began to confuse music and theory. When I graduated with a BA in music in 1977, I had a great G.P.A., but a tremendous amount of confusion about my musical identity."

"Now that's the first time you've used the word identity on this whole trip. You never identified yourself with Zen, or nature, or anything else?"

"No, never. I don't think kids really create an identity for themselves outside of their membership in a family. As we approach adulthood we

Chapter 6: Art & Authenticity

separate from our families, or our families separate from us, and we are forced to adopt a more individualized identity. With the level of dysfunction in my family I clung to music like a life raft. I really wanted to be a musician, but kept barking up the wrong trees in search of success, instead of working and training to discover my own affinities within music. Later in life I discovered those affinities as well as recognizing my deficiencies, but by then it was too late to really pursue a career."

"So, if you could do it all over again, knowing then what you know now, would you have been more successful at music?"

"I doubt it. Don't forget those deficiencies, which I still carry. But I also believe that things happen for a reason; that we are sometimes propelled in a certain direction, or sometimes diverted from a certain direction, in order to stay on a particular trajectory in our lives."

"So, are identity and trajectory the same thing?"

"Hmm. I never thought of it that way, but . . . yeah, I suppose so . . . I think so. And, since it appears we can choose a different trajectory, can we alter our basic identity as well? I tried most of my adult life to create a trajectory and an identity as a musician—'I am a musician'—and yet that trajectory, which had a major impact in propelling me to where I am today, didn't ultimately create that identity. Today I am still very much an amateur musician, but have become a professional minister. So, I take it back: trajectory and identity are not the same, but they are intertwined. And I think both trajectory and identity can be authentic or inauthentic depending on how they resonate with the deepest authentic self."

I felt like I might have talked us into a philosophical cul-de-sac, and Alan was looking a little pensive too. Finally he spoke, "Being authentic seems to be at the core of something—of your identity and trajectory? Yet you seemed to be discovering a lack of authenticity through music during your college years?"

"Actually, you haven't heard the half of it. I graduated from Cal. State Hayward in 1977, when Disco music was beginning to make it big, and I couldn't imagine a more inauthentic form of music than Disco. I really, really hated it. So much for eclecticism, huh? I took a year off from school, just bumming around, working jobs in warehouses, that kind of thing, and then in September of 1978 I enrolled at the University of California, San Diego to try and get my MA degree in music composition. Once again, I did what I thought I should do because I had no sense at all of what I wanted to do. I think of my two years there like being on a bus that you

Part II: Dissonance

boarded with enthusiasm and confidence at a known bus stop, but find that you are completely lost and at sea when you finally disembark in a dark alley at the end of the line. You took a journey but you ended up nowhere. Like I said, these weren't really the best years of my life."

"The search for authenticity led you through a musical swamp?"

"You have no idea. For example, the second year I was there, there was a lot of excitement over the fact that John Cage would be on campus and we would be premiering some of his works."

"Who's John Cage?"

"Oh, you truly are illiterate! In the 1950s, John Cage was *the* pioneer of avant-garde music. In his most famous piece, a pianist comes out and sits at the piano bench for four minutes and thirty seconds of silence.[1] Very avant-garde, very intellectual, and he continued in this vein his whole career. He became the herald and spokesperson for aleatonic music."

"Is that like absolute music?"

"It is the exact opposite of absolute music. Aleatonic music is music created by chance; like picking the notes of a song by rolling dice. Although earlier composers had experimented with aleatonic music, Cage really brought it to the forefront of avant-garde music in the early 1950s. So, by the late seventies, he not only remained very well-known, he was also very much imitated. He had spawned a whole industry of otherwise talentless composers competing with each other to create the wackiest and most pretentious pieces of 'music' you could imagine."

"Try me."

"Okey dokey. One of my compatriots at UCSD dreamed up this idea of using snails to create music. I kid you not. The idea was to put beams of light through the terrarium where the snails were, like the beam you break when you walk into a store that sets off a tone. The beams would be attached to boxes that made different tones, so that when the snails crawled around in the terrarium, they would break the beams and set off different tones, producing gastropod induced aleatonic music."

Alan, of course, burst out laughing. "So, how did that go?"

"Well, the big night came when all the students would be presenting their compositions, and my colleague dutifully brought out the terrarium full of snails and turned on the beams. The audience fell into an incredulous silence, awaiting *Le Suite Escargot*. Yet silent it remained. It turns out, snails

---

1. The proper title of this work is *4'33"*, and it can be performed by any combination of instruments and vocalists.

Chapter 6: Art & Authenticity

can suffer from stage fright just like humans, and in the pressure of the moment they succumbed to performance anxiety and remained stationary, firmly retreating into their shells and refusing to venture out through the beams. But here's the kicker: my colleague received an 'A' on that assignment, even as the snails lost their professional careers and were returned to the garden." I shook my head. "Life's not fair!"

"And yet, you paid good money to attend that school."

"And I found all of that just as tiresome as Disco. However, I assumed that because all of John Cage's imitators were so craven and insincere—and snail abusers to boot—John Cage himself must be the most craven and insincere of all. It turned out that I was wrong.

"When I first met him, eyeing him suspiciously at a rehearsal, it was immediately apparent that he had the charm and intelligence that often accompanied such an original thinker. And as we rehearsed—yes, you do still have to rehearse aleatonic music, as oxymoronic as that sounds—as we rehearsed, it became apparent that he was absolutely sincere and committed artistically to what he was doing. While I still can't say that I enjoyed his 'compositions' very much, I could tell he was working from his own, authentic voice. It was a weird voice, to be sure, but it was nevertheless authentic.

"It also turned out that this giant of the avant-garde music world had an obsession with the very prosaic game of bridge. My roommates and I had been teaching ourselves bridge, and Cage eagerly accepted our invitation to come over and fill in as our fourth. I think he liked being back in the messy, disorganized home of college students, and he absolutely wiped the floor with us! He was a cutthroat, take-no-prisoners contract bridge player, and we enjoyed every minute of it. And he too thought the whole snail idea was pretty stupid; he would have used animals that were much more likely to move and were more beautiful, like birds.

"It was a pretty important lesson in making judgments about what is authentic and what is not. I was studying with well-respected music professors, two of whom would go on to win Pulitzer prizes, yet found them lacking in authenticity as they tried to succeed in the University system. Yet this wacky guy from way, way out in left field who was writing music I didn't at all care for convinced me of his authenticity. What was the difference? I mean, at the end of the day I didn't like any of their music, so authenticity doesn't seem to be tied to outcomes. And Cage wasn't even remotely like Suzuki-roshi, though he had an interest in Zen, yet they both struck me the

Part II: Dissonance

same way as having some inner-core, some unsullied area of the soul that propelled them to do what they did."

"Unsullied or unmasked?"

"It could be both or either, don't you think? A place at some distinct moment in time that is free from disillusionment, no matter how that happened. Maybe unmasked by a rattlesnake and fear for a brief moment, or left unsullied from birth. Maybe unmasked by love or peeled back like an onion to remain unsullied going forward. Unsullied as a child: a child cannot help but be authentic, even if that is to the great distraction of his parents. Later, masked over by life and lies and disappointment, only to be unearthed again later by—what? I think many people stay covered up by life and lies and disappointments, and never find their—what?"

For some reason, Alan looked angry at this. Did he think I was secretly accusing him of never finding his—what? As we approached the outskirts of Boise I realized that I didn't really know what Alan's—what?—was. For a day and a half he had been grilling me, which I guess had been our agreement, but I hadn't taken any opportunities to return fire. I was about to do so when he sighed and asked, "Didn't anything good come of your experience in grad school?"

"You know, I left there completely disillusioned about modern classical music. It seemed completely phony to me; all mind and no heart. I still feel that way. University generated music seems quite inauthentic to me. Like they've all missed the point. Here's another example. I took a music theory and analysis course, and we were assigned the task of analyzing the music from Debussy's ballet *Jeux*. The ballet is about a seemingly innocent game of French Doubles, but when the tennis ball is lost things get more and more heated, finally ending in a very famous and very scandalous triple kiss. Ooo-la-la! Anyway, the music is gorgeous, and we all diligently sat down to try and construct some kind of analysis for this thing. And we couldn't. It simply defied every analytical technique we could think of. When you heard a theme in the second half you thought 'surely I heard that in the first half,' but you'd go back and look for it in the score and you simply couldn't find it. Debussy was a master of misdirection and disguise in his music.

"As it so happened the famous French composer Betsy Jolas was in town. She held the Chair of Analysis at the Paris *Conservatoire*, and we prevailed on our professor to invite her to come to our class and give us her take on *Jeux*. Surely, the person who held the Chair of Analysis at the

Chapter 6: Art & Authenticity

Paris *Conservatoire* ought to be able to give a good accounting of Debussy's masterpiece. She graciously accepted our invitation and came up to the university to give an hour talk on Debussy and *Jeux*. After she left, we all looked at each other, including the professor, and said, 'Nah. She doesn't get it either.'

"Debussy supposedly once said, 'Without mystery, there is no music.' This was the point that I felt everyone in the university was missing: they simply couldn't accept that there is an ineffable yet essential aspect to music, an aspect that defies analysis. And later on, this became a shared learning for me, a concept transfer, because surely 'without mystery, there is no God.' As hard as we try to understand, there remains an ineffable and essential aspect to God. Just as we poor music students wasted hours trying to crack the mysteries of *Jeux*, so do we needlessly spend lifetimes trying to intellectually understand God. In both cases we would be better off simply trying to live into the mystery, to embrace it, and to co-create with it. We can experience *Jeux* in all of it luscious glory, but we can't really explain it. Analogously, we can experience God but not really explain God. The mystery is the source of authenticity in music, and it is also what makes God real. The mystery can be described, yes, but analyzed, no; a fact that drives both systematic theologians and musical theorists crazy. Anyway, that realization surrounding *Jeux* gave me perhaps the most valuable take away from my years in university music training."

I looked at Alan and could tell that all of this had gone in one ear and out the other. I suspected this, like so much of our conversation, was going to be deflected, and I was not disappointed.

"Really?" he said. "The head of the Paris *Conservatoire* is the best you can do? That was the most important thing that happened to you in college?"

"What do you mean?" I asked cautiously.

"C'mon, dude. You were in college. You were in college in a beach town! But apparently, instead of getting laid, you were playing bridge with snails and fantasizing about triple kisses. I can see why you thought music had lost its magic."

I laughed nervously. I wanted to continue along my philosophical lines, but apparently things had gotten too arcane for Alan. Would he ever hear any of this? Finally I said, "You're just deflecting off the question of authenticity."

"Which," he countered, "is very authentic of me. And look who's deflecting. My guess is that you felt like most everything sucked primarily

Part II: Dissonance

because your love life sucked. So I am pruriently interested, seeing as how we're traversing this spiritual desert of yours, in finding out why your love life sucked."

"I thought you didn't want to hear about all of that stuff."

"Well, now I do."

"Okey dokey." As we sped down I-84 through the tumbleweeds of southern Idaho, I caved into Alan's previously veiled interest in my love life, and rapidly changed the subject as if we had suddenly flown off the highway onto dirt and gravel. I suspected we were about to crash.

Chapter 7: Relationships & Religion

"I WAS AT UCSD from 1978 to 1980, a part of the seventies era that has been referred to as 'The Golden Age of Sex.' In that post-birth control pill, pre-AIDS world, a lot of people were having a lot of sex with a lot of partners. I wasn't one of them."

Alan sniggered briefly, and I had to laugh a little nervously.

"Hey, give me a break! I had this big vacancy in my heart from my family relationships, and in an era that valued quantity over quality, that vacancy demanded quality. It created in me a romantic and naïve notion that before I slept with a girl, I ought to at least be nominally in love with her, and she with me. Consequently, although I fell in love with every pretty girl I met, they for the most part were not so obliging and I spent much of my late teens and early twenties lonely and desperate for love. This state of affairs was frustrating and out of step with the times, but I later came to see it as a blessing. Focusing on quantity would just have been piling more dysfunction on top of the already substantial relational dysfunction I had grown up with."

Now Alan just laughed outright. "Bravo! That's the first time I've ever heard a straight man admit that his inability to get a girl was actually a blessing!"

"Thanks for the support," I said sarcastically. "So anyway, when I met Pamela in 1976, I recklessly ignored the obvious warning signs of incompatibility simply because she said she loved me. We were able to develop an illusion of a functional relationship, and I developed the illusion that the vacancy had been filled. In another of life's little ironies it was my old high school girlfriend Julie, who had long since moved on to greener pastures, who introduced me to Pamela. When your old girlfriend introduces you to your new girlfriend, this should be a hint of the train-wreck that is coming.

"Since you have so gleefully demonstrated a penchant for the prurient, I am *not* going to divulge all of the intimate secrets of my love life with my first wife Pamela—or anyone else. . ."

"Shoot!"

". . . But that relationship *is* a relevant thread among all those that led me to ordination, and disastrous as our relationship was, it ultimately helped me to at least partially fill some of that vacancy inherited from my upbringing. Because of the emotional distance of my father, and my mother's increasing anger about her marriage, I had no idea about the importance of healthy relationships in a family, or with anyone else for that matter. Put simply, I didn't know how to *do* relationships. I had no healthy model to follow, and was taught at home that relationships should be awkward, with long stretches of emotional demilitarized zones regularly interrupted by periods of high drama. Having subsequently studied family dynamics I can see all of this glaring dysfunction now, but like all of the other threads I've discussed, this type of non-relationship was simply baked in as 'normal' in my family. This was what I brought to the table in my relationship with Pamela and it formed my contribution to our ultimate downfall.

"One factor in this approach to relationships lay with the spiritual atmosphere in my family as I was growing up. Zen Buddhism is not particularly concerned with relationships: there is no anthropomorphized god with whom to form a human-divine relationship, and the seeking of enlightenment is a personal spiritual discipline. This is not to say that Buddhist temples or Japanese society in general do not have relationship forming components, but Zen in particular focuses on the individual's practice that leads to the individual's enlightenment. The Judeo-Christian heritage, on the other hand, strongly emphasizes relationship, from Adam and Eve, God and Job, all the way down to one's own relationship with God through Jesus Christ."

"So are you saying that there are no Zen potlucks?"

I laughed. "Not really. The Los Altos *zendo* folks tried to have breakfasts after sitting *zazen*, and they were trying to implement a laity type of Zen rather than a cloistered, monastic type, so it did include a social component. Mom socialized with many of the people who were a part of the *zendo*, but the two weren't really linked the way they are in a typical American Protestant church. For one thing, Buddhists don't really proselytize—they

Chapter 7: Relationships & Religion

don't actively seek new converts. This has its positive side—no religious arm-twisting—but it also has the down side of not promoting relationships in a spiritual context. Still, regardless of what other people may have been doing, Mom used Zen as another way to isolate herself from her family. In a Protestant church, she might have availed herself of the casual social gatherings that take place after church and encourage a familial communalism. She probably could have done the same at the *zendo*, but the impetus wasn't really there to encourage that.

"Even in Japan, Zen is considered a little arcane; something for the specialists to do. Imagine if Christianity had been introduced in Japan only through the lens of Trappist monks. It would be authentic, but rather specialized in its implementation. Many Americans, including my mother, were introduced to Buddhism as seen through the lens of Zen; again, authentic, but specialized. Just as most Christians are not monks, Trappist or otherwise, most Buddhists do not practice Zen. And just as in the West we tend to keep our religious specialists cloistered, so do Buddhists like to keep theirs as well. But Suzuki-roshi was trying to establish an everyday sort of Zen practice for non-cloistered, non-specialized followers which created, I think, a double collision: East versus West and specialist versus laity.

"So, while Buddhism in general may indeed include all of the social trappings encapsulated in a potluck, Zen is not particularly oriented in that way. In some ways, Zen was a movement to return a certain original purity to Buddhist practice, which definitely included the Buddha's focus on individual enlightenment, and lack of focus on social issues. That at least was the message I received unconsciously when observing my mother's Zen practice and interactions, and this created in me a kind of non-congruity of how relationships and spirit worked together. They were different in my day to day living than they were in the unarticulated practice my mom was doing, and this introduced problems I was not aware of in my own relationships. Misinterpreting this cultural expectation had become a part of my own spiritual DNA. I suspect that my issues were mostly symptoms of the collisions that were occurring between East and West in my own family circle. And I am not trying to say that devout Christian families can't be dysfunctional—clearly, they can—but that I was starting out with some baseline assumptions that my friends didn't share. This was not helpful when it came to forming the first adult relationship in my life."

"Wait a minute. Are you actually saying your mom's involvement with Zen Buddhism caused the dysfunction in your first marriage?"

Part II: Dissonance

"No, no; not directly anyway. I'm pretty sure the major cause of my contribution to the dysfunction in my first marriage was my parent's own dysfunctional marriage. But I can't help but think that if they had been involved together in a more relational spiritual life, had they attended some Methodist potlucks—or even some Buddhist potlucks—things might have gone better for them. But Mom, consciously or unconsciously, was actively working against that. The truth was, spiritual life and relationship seemed totally disconnected for my parents, and Zen didn't improve this disconnection. Sometimes it's just hard to say which is the cause and which is the effect, and to what degree of influence one has on the other. Nevertheless, I had almost no framework in which to form ideas about a healthy relationship. Who knows—maybe that even contributed to my skepticism about more relational religions? Possibly, but it certainly tainted my relationship with Pamela.

"Whether she and I should have ever gotten together in the first place is not completely irrelevant, since Pamela was at that time engaged to someone else. That this was a moral quandary never even occurred to me, and although it should have been another red flag concerning the future of our relationship, it became simply the first in a long string of dramas. Nevertheless, Pamela eventually broke off her engagement in order to be with me, and we began a 5 year courtship that led to our marriage in 1981. 'Courtship' makes it sound like a medieval romance: it was anything but. Those years were marked by infidelity on both our parts, Pamela's recreational drug use, significant time apart, and the grinding conflict between our careers and our relationship. I found myself in that poisonous trap of not really wanting to be with her, but not really believing I could find anyone else. An example of how little we related to each other, to this day I have no idea why she stayed with me: it was never discussed. All of this was part and parcel of the 'loser' mentality that comes with being an adult child of an alcoholic, as well as all of the other dysfunction that I've mentioned. It took me a long time to realize that the vacancy had not in fact been filled.

"Nevertheless, it was not all negative. In fact, two events happened because of this relationship that would later be seminal in bringing me to where I am today. Alan, we are still quite a ways from directly answering the questions you asked way back in Troutdale, but here at least are a couple of more tangible clues."

Alan sighed. "Well, I guess at the time I did ask for the long story. I'm beginning to wonder now if there's a Reader's Digest version?"

Chapter 7: Relationships & Religion

"Nope. In the fall of 1976 Pamela left for a nine month stay in France to work as an *au pair*—sort of a maid/student/nanny—with a family near Avignon. This was the first of several separations. But during the Christmas break of 1976 I flew, with Julie and her boyfriend Ron, to Europe to bum around for a month. When I say bum around, I mean it. None of us had any money to speak of. I had sold my car in order to buy the plane ticket, and we did everything on the cheap, including sleeping on trains at night so we wouldn't have to pay for hotel rooms. Pamela joined us in London, and the four of us began our trip by touring around England, Wales and Scotland. It was marvelous! Even in winter we loved the British countryside and the museums and attractions we could afford to get into. Our travels eventually took us to Bangor, Wales, where we spent the night in a Bed & Breakfast that was situated above a pub. Best beer I've ever had . . . Anyway, the next day we took a bus to Caernarvon and toured its famous castle where traditionally the Prince of Wales is crowned. Since the bus only ran in the morning and evening, by the afternoon we had some free time, and decided to take a walk through the surrounding countryside. It was wet and cold, but also marvelously exotic. The trees had long ago lost their leaves, and steam, like a Thule fog, drifted across the rolling fields. It had that feeling of being a country that had been inhabited for thousands of years, where the ground remembered every footfall. I think as Americans, where everything is new, we were particularly sensitive to that feeling.

"Soon we found ourselves on a dirt lane that ran out amongst the sheep pastures outside of town. Through the trees we could see the Menai Strait that bisects the peninsula, a blue and inviting counterpoint to the mossy green/grey winter countryside. Looking in towards a fenced sheep pasture we spotted what looked to be a stone circle in the distance. Being rude Americans, we hopped the fence and made our way to the center of the field, where indeed there was an old stone circle, overgrown with grass that the sheep were calmly trimming.

"Arriving at the middle of this small circle, I was suddenly struck by the same feeling I had had in the meadow at Pinecrest years before: this was a thin place! There was a spiritual humming that you could almost hear, and I realized that this ancient place had once hosted ceremonies and sacraments long before it was converted to a pasture. While Pamela, Julie and Ron trotted around snapping pictures, I stood transfixed in the center of the circle, feeling that I could almost commune with the very stones themselves. Outside of Stonehenge, I knew practically nothing about the

Part II: Dissonance

British indigenous cultures—which often get lumped together under the name 'Celtic'—or their spirituality; yet this direct communion with a Divine Presence required no intellectual knowledge or learning. We stayed there only for a brief time as we needed to hurry back so as not to miss the bus, but that memory has remained vivid in my mind ever since. That vividness would eventually play a key role in breaking the barriers I developed surrounding Christianity."

"Another bread crumb, O Hansel?"

"Another bread crumb. Seems like I'm leaving quite a mess behind me. The second seminal event was, oddly, the wedding itself. After years of issues, frustration and separateness, Pamela and I decided to double down on our dysfunction by officially tying the knot. We were once again living in Berkeley in the summer of 1981. Pamela's family had lived in Berkeley when she was younger, so she had a long association with a United Methodist Church in the Berkeley hills, near the Solano tunnel. We chose this church to be the site of our nuptials. I had previously worked in other Methodist churches as a choir director, but this was the first time I had really interacted with the congregation and, more importantly, the pastor. Kyle Morton was a textbook Methodist pastor: well educated, affable and wise, a good family man and a faithful servant of the church. I liked that church primarily because of its active music program, including a complete five octave set of bells, but Kyle became the first Christian to have even the slightest positive influence on my spiritual development. And slight it was, but you 'must have a beginning, you know.'[1] For one thing, I began to see that church as a place of healthy relationships, which was kind of an eye-opener for me, and these included a healthy relationship with God exemplified by the pastor. And yes, I did attend several potlucks there. It's amazing how something as mundane as a potluck gathering can have such an influence.

"The wedding ceremony itself was ridiculous. We read bad original poetry to each other as well as shallow made-up vows. Mom later told me that she had to keep sucking on Lifesavers in order to keep herself from breaking out in laughter. Nevertheless, it did take place in a church and we were obliged to say some of the Christian words. No matter how much you justify yourself by claiming *they're just words*, when they are spoken aloud they have meaning whether you want them to or not. They didn't sink in as

---

1. There is a Gilbert & Sullivan quote for almost any circumstance in life. This one is spoken by Pitti-Sing from *The Mikado*.

Chapter 7: Relationships & Religion

our marriage quickly disintegrated, but they did hang around, hiding in my subconscious, until they could be activated later on.

"Pamela and I moved into a little rental home in San Jose, where we both farted around for a while, with each other and with our non-existent careers. We might have gone on like that forever, but two more events happened that finally brought our relationship to an end. In 1982 Pamela discovered that she was pregnant. She decided that a baby was not a part of her 'master plan,' though I doubt she actually had a 'master plan'; and I, having no sense of fatherhood or responsibility, just went along with Pamela's decision. On a warm summer day I drove Pamela to a clinic in Sunnyvale where the child was aborted. Again, the lack of consciousness about anything resembling a moral center was apparent in the casualness with which I agreed to this procedure. Was the moral center there, but just masked? I suspect so, because as far as I know, this is the only event in my life which I buried so deep I actually believed for years that it had never happened. Something deeply wrong had occurred, something had struck that unconscious moral center, and I had no facilities whatsoever to deal with it. I never even thought about the moral consequences of what we were doing, regardless of whether we would go through with it or not. I don't think Pamela did either, and this drove an invisible and unspoken wedge into our marriage. I'm not trying to make a definitive statement about abortion here, but I think that unborn child haunted my subconscious for years.

"But the final straw came in the fall of that same year. Pamela had decided that she had really loved her time in France, and decided to go back and spend another year there—without me. Our inchoate thinking patterns about what constituted a healthy relationship hadn't changed or improved one bit since we had gotten married. One day I was in our living room helping Pamela pack some boxes, when I came to a complete stop. I couldn't move and I couldn't speak, and sank down to the floor, nearly in the same darkness that had overtaken me when I had to put our dog to sleep in Los Altos. Since my consciousness was completely incapable of expressing my deep anxiety about Pamela leaving for a year, my subconscious took over and just simply shut down the system. Reboot. After a while, I finally was able to convey to Pamela that I didn't want her to go, and she agreed to cancel her trip. I'm sure she deeply resented this. But it really was too little, too late, and although we stubbornly remained married until 1985, the relationship really had expired on that day. It had started badly, gone badly and

Part II: Dissonance

would end badly. But from its ashes would come a new and much improved era in relationships, both with women and with God."

"At last!" Alan said eagerly. "Here comes the red head!"

Again I laughed. "You've always had a thing for her, haven't you?" Alan nodded guiltily. "Well, it might surprise you, and perhaps even disappoint you to learn that she wasn't always a red head. In the spring of 1983 I was at an audition for the Gilbert & Sullivan operetta *The Gondoliers* for the Gilbert & Sullivan Society of San Jose. The auditions were well underway and I was waiting my turn, when suddenly a whirlwind of blonde hair flew into the room, had a loud and brief argument with the director, then blew out again. She was an Apparition.[2] I had no idea what they had argued about, but I did know that more than anything, I wanted to meet this whirlwind! I won a small part in the show, but The Apparition was not in the cast and it was several months before I saw her again.

"We were finally cast together in a subsequent production of *H.M.S. Pinafore*, and we became friends. Her hair had transformed into that copper-red that you inexplicably love so much—and, obviously, I do too—which made her that much more attractive. With our mutual friend Anne we would tootle around the Bay Area going to auditions for various opera and operetta companies. We would frequently go from these to Los Compadres Mexican restaurant in Hayward to celebrate our successes or mourn our failures with the best margaritas and enchiladas in the Bay Area. Since I was still technically married our relationship remained innocent, but that didn't stop us from developing a delicious flirtation. But once again, Alan, I am not going to tantalize you with the intimate details of my relationship with the red headed Apparition, Vivian."

"Darn!"

"Suffice it to say that as my marriage went downhill the flirtation began to develop into something more serious. We wanted to be with each other and got fairly creative at doing so—the theater is wonderful that way. Again, being the unconscious dolt that I was, even this serious flirtation with a woman not my wife wasn't a signal to me that something was deeply wrong. For a while I desperately clung to my marriage because I didn't want it to fail like my parents' had. However, fate intervened. In 1984 Vivian was waltzing through a field at a friend's house in Saratoga when she stepped into a gopher hole and managed to sever all the tendons between her knee

---

2. An apparition is sometimes thought of as a ghost, but I was thinking more of the Merriam-Webster definition: an "unusual or unexpected sight."

Chapter 7: Relationships & Religion

and her calf. She wound up in an ankle to thigh cast and had to move in with our friend Anne. I visited her regularly while she was in the hospital, and after she got out we would occasionally go up to that house in Saratoga. She would hobble up the steps while I followed with a bottle of wine, and we would sit on the porch and discuss just about everything.

"She was such a beautiful woman that I freely admit my initial attraction had much more to do with biology than theology. But I was also fascinated with someone whose background was so different from mine. She'd been raised a Methodist, but when a Methodist youth leader had told her that she didn't really have to believe in the resurrection, she wandered away, sensing a lack of spiritual depth in the Methodist church, and over the years she had tried several different spiritual paths. An example of her no-nonsense approach to spirituality came when she attended an EST seminar. EST—you know, Werner Erhard and that whole thing—was really just all about control. At this particular session they ushered Vivian and the rest of the crowd into a room and shut the doors, clearly explaining that no one could leave the room until they were told to, and if they did leave they couldn't come back. So, when Vivian got up to use the rest room and was told that she couldn't leave, she responded by saying calmly, 'Either I use the bathroom or I pee on your foot. Your choice . . .' While the EST trainer sputtered and tried to come up with a response, she walked out of the room and, just to make her point, came back in after using the restroom and completed the seminar.

"When she told me this story, I nearly fell off my chair in laughter, but it also awakened me to the idea that if you are going to submit to a spiritual master, be careful which master you pick. I had been so fortunate without even knowing it to have Suzuki-roshi as a model, and it was that difference in quality that really differentiated a cult from a legitimate spiritual path. Still, her stories reinforced my wariness of religious leaders. As these conversations with her continued I was inexorably hooked by biology, theology, philosophy—all three and more—all at once. But even deeper was the beginning of the sense that maybe I wasn't such a loser after all. It started with the miraculous revelation that a woman as stunningly beautiful as Vivian was falling in love with plain-old me, but it also came from the realization that I could hold my own in these conversations with the smartest person I'd ever met.

"Eventually I realized what an idiot I was and separated from Pamela, and Vivian and I were free to be in love. We continued to do Community

Part II: Dissonance

Theater together; operas sometimes, but mostly Gilbert and Sullivan operettas. Those were really good times."

"Well, after your soap-opera marriage to Pamela, tell me about life on stage with the Apparition."

I laughed a little self-consciously. "There are way too many stories to tell, but here's one of my favorites. One time we were in a production of *H.M.S. Pinafore*, and Vivian was playing the role of Josephine, the Captain's daughter. The costumer had decided to create a very . . . uh . . . revealing, low cut costume for Vivian. He claimed he was just trying to sell seats in the balcony. Anyway, the costume required some specialty undergarments to keep everything in its proper place. During one performance I, playing the role of Ralph the strapping foremast hand, glided across the stage towards Josephine when I heard a distinct rustling sound, like paper being crumpled. Vivian also looked particularly pained, something quite odd for a woman who was a real natural on stage. I found out after the show that she had suffered a catastrophic wardrobe malfunction with those specialty undergarments, and the costumer, desperate for a solution, ended up using masking tape to strap her into place. To this day, I can't tape up a package without her cringing and clutching her bosom."

"Oh, no! You're just making that up!" I could tell Alan was getting a little excited imagining all of this.

"Well, maybe the last part," I laughed, "but the part about the masking tape is true. You could hear the screams from her dressing room after the show as she got out of her costume."

"Sheesh." Alan paused for a moment. "What a change from Pamela."

"It was night and day. And Vivian passed the ultimate test when I took her to meet my mother. Mom was living in Bolinas at that time, in a little rental seaside cottage almost completely enveloped with bougainvillea. It was really quite lovely and cozy, very coast of New England-like in that weird little town south of Point Reyes. It was a one minute walk from her house to the beach and you could see the Golden Gate Bridge and most of San Francisco to the southeast, and miles and miles of glittering-blue ocean to the south and west. Vivian was, naturally, a little nervous about meeting my mom, but the two of them hit it off immediately. Mom had never really liked Pamela, but she took to Vivian like a second daughter. I was getting a little smarter by then and realized this was a good sign."

"Isn't Bolinas way out in the middle of nowhere? Why was your mom living out there?"

Chapter 7: Relationships & Religion

"Bolinas is actually at the far end of nowhere. In fact, it's on an entirely different continental plate than the rest of the U.S. We used to joke that if the big earthquake finally hit California, San Francisco and L.A. might sink into the ocean, but Bolinas and Point Reyes would be just fine. It was a real hippie town in the early 1980s. Grace Slick, the lead singer for the Jefferson Airplane, had a house there, and it was one of those places populated mostly by wealthy eccentrics and struggling artists. That, of course, was irresistible to my mom. A friend of hers had told her that he had a place to rent to her in Bolinas, and she loved it." I paused for a minute. "Her residency there was, I'm afraid, all too short."

"Why? What happened?"

Again, I had to pause. Finally I said, "Look, it's getting pretty late, and I'm starving. Let's find a Denny's or something and get some dinner." We were just getting into the north end of the Great Salt Lake, passing through Tremonton and heading south towards Brigham City. The ushering darkness seemed fitting for the next chapter, but it simply could not be told on a growling stomach. The mood in the car had changed suddenly as well, from the silly joy of falling in love to the nervousness of an unknown future.

Alan grunted. "Well, OK then. But please, not Denny's. Anything but Denny's."

"Anything?"

We passed a couple of exits with a variety of fast food places advertised, but finally pulled into the Denny's in Ogden. I told Alan to just imagine it was a Shari's and he agreed glumly as we trooped in for dinner.

75

Chapter 8: Nexus I

NIGHT SETTLES LIKE SMOG on the basin of the Great Salt Lake. Maybe there were just a lot of wood burning stoves, or maybe it was the mist coming off the lake, but every time I passed through this area at night the darkness seemed heavy, unlike the clear, crisp nights of the high country of Colorado that I loved so much. Alan and I had carried on a desultory conversation over dinner, mostly about nothing. A Seinfeld dinner. Uncharacteristically we both turned down an offer of Dutch Apple Pie from "Rachel: Service with a Smile!", so after using the restroom and a quick stop to refill the gas tank, we hurried back to the freeway.

"Mom and Dad separated in 1975, but they never actually got divorced." I blurted out as we accelerated up the on-ramp. We were heading south on I-15, but would never actually make it to Salt Lake City. Instead, we'd be taking the I-84 bypass in Ogden and heading up Morgan Valley before getting on I-80 eastbound toward Evanston, Wyoming. By day it was a beautiful drive; by night it was just freeway. When Alan didn't respond, I got the sense that he was just going to listen for a while.

"A few months after Mom left, while Dad was selling the home in Los Altos out from under us, she was diagnosed with uterine cancer and had to undergo a complete hysterectomy. Dad dutifully came to visit her, and she was too weak to turn him away, but it was pointless. During all those years and all those hospital visits, we never once realized that drunken-ole-Dad was still working and keeping his medical insurance to pay for all of this. In that I feel guilty and sorry for him. But nevertheless, Mom wanted nothing to do with him. She moved into a little house in Ladera and Dad moved into an apartment in San Carlos. The great détente had begun.

Chapter 8: Nexus I

"Mom seemed to want many of the things she had missed out on as a housewife, including a satisfying relationship with a man. Somehow or another she met a charming Englishman named Peter, and she began acting like a giddy schoolgirl on her first date. Their relationship was completely platonic, and one evening she came over to my apartment in Hayward and explained to me why. Twenty years old and counseling my mother on her love life was something I was completely unprepared for, not the least when she told me, between big sobs, that Peter was gay and they would never be lovers. I was speechless. This was way, way beyond my comfort zone, but I stuck it out and tried to provide some comfort for Mom. Nevertheless, it was Peter who owned the house in Bolinas and offered it to my mom to rent. Mom's resources consisted solely of whatever meager support Dad provided her, but it was apparently enough. So, at some point in 1977, she moved out to Bolinas.

"Life in Bolinas really suited Mom. She made friends with some of the rich eccentrics who lived up on the bluffs above town, and mingled with the poor artists in town, of which she was one. After years of painting in the black and white style of *sumi-e*, Mom broke out the chalk, oils and crayons, and armed with a vivid, colorful palette she began creating whimsical beach and ocean scenes. She also joined in with the local theater group and proudly painted a backdrop for their production of *The Mikado*.[1] The mountain backdrop looked like a combination of Mt. Tamalpais, which looms over Marin County, and Mt. Fuji in Japan; it was dubbed Mt. Fujipais. This may have been the happiest time in my mother's life. She seemed to like living an isolated life, behind a gate and walls of bougainvillea. She had very little interest in being a grandmother when Norm and his wife, and later Hattie Lou and her husband, produced children.

"Dad, on the other hand, continued to struggle with alcoholism. Living in his little apartment afforded him the opportunity to drink alone and with impunity. Although we were never quite sure, we think his employer, Varian Assoc., asked him to take early retirement. It's really a testament to the kind of corporate loyalty that existed back then that they kept him on as long as they did. Dad cashed out of his retirement fund and bought himself a cabin in the woods a few miles outside of Murphys. Murphys is about twenty miles east of Angels Camp in the California gold country.

---

1. One of my mom's Japanese friends was highly insulted that she helped with a production of *The Mikado* until she pointed out "it's really poking fun at English people, not the Japanese!" Amazingly, this mollified her friend.

77

Part II: Dissonance

We didn't see a lot of each other, but Dad's life seemed divided between splitting wood, drinking, and going to AA meetings. We still had the cabin at Pinecrest which all of us kids used pretty regularly, but I think it was just another burden to Dad.

"This standoff lasted until 1981, when Mom was diagnosed with lymphoma. This is a very serious and aggressive form of cancer. In today's world some successful treatments have been found; in 1981, it was pretty much a sentence of torture by radiation and chemo, followed by death. I didn't know what to do, and I don't think my siblings did either, since we had all been raised to accept dysfunctional relationships as the norm. We tried to ignore it, and looking back now I can see that Mom relied on her Bolinas friends a lot for rides into San Francisco for treatments. After two years she had a brief remission, but then the cancer returned with a vengeance and it became simply a matter of time.

"It is difficult to understand the human heart, or to condense human behavior into nicely predictable patterns. When it became apparent that Mom could no longer live alone, Dad offered to build an extension on to his house in Murphys, complete with a sunlit painting studio, if Mom would come and live with him. I knew what my Dad's motivation was: he just wanted her back. But I almost fell off my chair when Mom told me she had accepted his offer. 'Why?' I asked. 'He's a drunk, and you couldn't stand living with him.'

"Mom smiled, wanly, and said, 'When all is said and done, he's been my best friend for almost forty years. And when all is said and done, he'll take care of me.'

"I realized then that I was twenty-seven years old and didn't know anything about love. For once, and maybe for the only time, my parents had taught me something about the value of commitment, and the power of love to overcome just about anything. And you know, I didn't realize it until just now, but when Mom made that decision is when I made the decision to leave Pamela once and for all to pursue a much more real love with Vivian. Both of these events managed to relieve me of my cynicism concerning affairs of the heart.

"It took Dad several months to get the addition put on his house, but finally in December of 1984 Mom moved in, with all of her art supplies, and once again my parents were living together. Vivian and I went to visit them for Christmas, and Mom, pale and ill from her treatments, maintained her cutthroat style of Scrabble and whupped Vivian and me relentlessly. Her

Chapter 8: Nexus I

studio was lovely, with skylights in the ceiling and surrounded by windows that looked out into the forest. Nevertheless, her art supplies lay untouched, some moving boxes never opened. She was simply too sick to paint.

"Vivian and I returned to the Bay Area and our jobs, but in mid-February, I received 'the call': Mom was in the hospital, and she only had a little while left to live. I asked my boss for time off, and when this was denied I simply quit the job and drove up to Angels Camp, where Mom was in the hospital named after her favorite author, Mark Twain. Vivian was in the final rehearsals for a show that she was starring in and stayed behind. I stayed at Dad's house in Murphys, and was later joined by Hattie Lou and Charlie. Norm, who had become a National Park Ranger, lived in Nevada at the time and visited for a few days before going back to be with his wife and family. So, the four of us—I, Charlie, Hattie Lou and Dad—took turns sitting with Mom while the doctors and nurses pumped her full of chemo and morphine.

"In her last days, Mom had her cogent periods, in spite of being completely bald and physically emaciated. During one of these semi-conscious moments she asked me to read to her. 'What?' I asked, hoping that there was some Mark Twain or John Steinbeck handy. Instead, much to my shock and surprise, she asked me to read from the Bible. I went into full panic mode. These might be the last words my mother would ever hear, and I had absolutely no clue what to read. I had barely ever opened a Bible in my life, but desperately thumbed my way to the one section of the Bible I recognized: the Twenty-third Psalm. I began to read:

'The Lord is my shepherd, I shall not want . . .'

"Mom's eyes opened wide and she roared, 'Nooooo!' and fell back into bed, exhausted. I began to cry: my one shot at providing comfort, and apparently I had blown it badly. I realize now that Mom wanted one of the great adventure stories—David or Moses or Elijah—or maybe even Jesus raising Lazarus from the dead. I didn't know any of those stories, didn't even know where to find them in the Bible, and I glumly put the Bible down and slunk out of the room.

"Fortunately, God provides for redemption. When I came back to the hospital for my next shift, Mom was actually pretty conscious and alert. I know now that this was that burst of energy that many people get a day or a few hours before they die: the *surge*. But whatever the reason, it was during this last conversation that Mom gave me the conundrum that led me to where I am today. Listen to this carefully, Alan, it's a gigantic bread crumb.

Part II: Dissonance

"Mom and I at first talked of inconsequential things, but after a while I asked her why she had asked me to read from the Bible. She told me something I had not known, that she had been brought up as a Christian Scientist. She had abandoned this faith early on, in part because her mother was so strange, and in part because she saw some of their practices as being destructive. But, since I have been trying to make the point since Portland that our childhood experiences have deep and lasting influence on our lives, apparently some semblance of the Christian faith had stuck with her. I asked her if she had found satisfaction in Zen Buddhism, her adopted faith. To my great dismay, she answered, 'No. Neither Christianity nor Buddhism ultimately provided me with complete satisfaction. I have never been able to find a religion that combined the active principles of Christianity with the meditative principles of Buddhism.'

"What had been ingrained in me as a child, unconsciously, now came rushing to the fore, and I saw that this conundrum had left Mom feeling spiritually abandoned. The logic was simple and obvious: to live a satisfying life one must combine spiritual discovery, through meditation and/or prayer, with service to others. Mom had never found a community that did this, only those that did one or the other."

"Wow," said Alan, finally bursting the bubble. "It sounds like you took that as some sort of commissioning, some sort of quest."

"It gnawed at me over time. I was, and still am, so distressed that my mom died without resolution to something that was deeply meaningful to her. And yet . . . and yet . . ." Suddenly I was far away and long ago. "The manner of her passing may have released her from that particular bond, as death releases us from so many."

"How so?"

I immediately regretted my musings. Having transported myself into the past, I had barely noticed that we were entering the Morgan Valley along I-84. The lights of Ogden disappeared behind us but the heavy darkness remained. I didn't tell very many people about what happened on the night my mother died; another night of heavy darkness followed by blinding light, so many years ago. It was too weird, even though it was one of the most powerful experiences of my life. Alan already thought I was a little off-center anyway: would telling him of a mystical experience reveal a foundational honesty, or would it reinforce his view that I was already a little 'koo-koo' and getting more so by the minute.

Chapter 8: Nexus I

"Earth to Major Tom. This is ground control. Are you still with us, Major Tom?"

I shook my head, and thought, *What the hell.*

"I was just thinking that the night Mom died was one of the strangest I have ever experienced. We knew by then that the end was near. Charlie had taken the evening shift at the hospital, and I was supposed to relieve him at 11 p.m. I was sleeping in my mother's studio at Dad's house, and had set an old heirloom alarm clock for 10 p.m. so I could get a little nap. The old heirloom, which had never failed before, did not go off, and when I awoke, it was almost midnight. I threw on some clothes and jumped into the car.

"Highway 4 is the main road from Murphys to Angels Camp, but there was a back road that was faster for getting to the hospital. There was a little bit of moon, just enough to add to the spookiness of the night. The road to the hospital had a unique feature. There was a wooden slough that ran next to the road, and the water in it appeared to be running uphill. It was a fun optical illusion by day; at night under the faltering rays of the half moon, it just added to the general sense of eeriness and unease that I felt.

"I finally got to the hospital and dashed up to Mom's room. I entered quietly, and noticed that Mom had started moaning rhythmically, in her sleep. Charlie was a little freaked out by this and was glad I had finally gotten there to relieve him. He left the room, and I sat down, alone with my dying mother in the dark. The emaciated, bald headed lady in the bed bore a remarkable resemblance to Suzuki-roshi, and very little to my mother. I realized at once that she was not just moaning randomly; she was trying to chant as she had done during *zazen* so many years before. I closed my eyes and, picking up her rhythm, began chanting with her.

"During the days leading up to her death, my sister and I had noticed Mom brushing something off her wrist, and we both came to the conclusion that there was an angel sitting there waiting to take Mom away, and that Mom did not want to go. As I chanted with Mom that night, the Angel appeared to me in a vision. It wasn't a white, fluffy angel, but instead was an old sea captain, grizzled and rumpled, who was rowing a boat to retrieve Mom. He wore a crumpled blue sailor's cap, and he looked annoyed, probably because Mom had been brushing him off for days. Suddenly, the Captain transformed into a bright light. Mom and I were taken up into the light, towards an aperture in the sky. As we approached the aperture the Angel, now beautiful and white, said to me in a stern voice: 'You cannot follow here.'

Part II: Dissonance

"I was startled and my eyes opened. The world and everything in it had gone silent, the hospital room frozen in time as Mom's soul departed this sphere. I had stopped breathing, and so had Mom, and I waited in respectful silence as she left the room. Then, I once again closed my eyes, and was surprised that the vision had not yet concluded. In a brief vignette there was Mom, a young girl, standing on the beach in Bolinas. The wind tousled her long hair as a gentle breeze blew in from the ocean which glistened behind her. Without saying a word, she turned and ran up the beach, and was gone.

"I sat in that stillness for I don't know how long. I was startled as Mom's body, unwilling to let go, gasped two breaths ten minutes apart, then finally lay still. A nurse came in and, pulling the sheet over her, said simply, 'Goodbye, Barbara.' The spell was broken, and I went out into the lobby to call my Dad and then called Vivian."

There was a long, long silence as the valley rushed around us. The same wan moon hung over the tips of the Wasatch Mountains that had glimmered in Angels Camp in the Sierras on that night twenty-eight years ago, and the lights of farmhouses seemed frozen in midair as we passed. Finally, Alan spoke.

"Man. That was quite a vivid hallucination."

"It wasn't an hallucination," I said, too quickly and too sharply.

"Hey, hey man, I'm sorry. I mean, losing your mother is hard, very hard. Emotions run high, very high and, you know, and the mind creates images to, you know, help you cope . . . but it was *just* an hallucination, you know"

I knew I never should have mentioned this to Alan. He was certainly right about high emotions though, and I sat for a few moments in silence to try to get mine under control. Why was Alan baiting me? I tried to respond without rising to the bait.

"In *Zen and the Art of Motorcycle Maintenance* Phaedrus, the main character, asks his colleagues at the University for their thoughts on 'quality.' He couldn't seem to get a handle on what the word 'quality' meant, so he asked other learned professors how they would define the word. After some pondering on their part, they came back and said, 'Oh, quality is just what you like.' This answer really bugged Phaedrus for a while, until he figured out that the problem with that answer was the word 'just.' By using that word, the idea of quality is belittled; the word is used as a pejorative. When the sentence is restructured as 'quality is what you like,' a whole world of mind expanding ideas opened up for Phaedrus. When 'quality'

Chapter 8: Nexus I

was no longer belittled, it began to form in his mind a central concept in human meaning.

"So, when you say my experience was 'just an hallucination' you belittle what an hallucination is. But, like Phaedrus, when you say, 'it was an hallucination,' you open up a much larger field for interpretation by acknowledging the importance of the event. In our scientific society we seem only interested in ascribing reality to things that can be measured, or that can be discerned through observation. We ascribe reality only to the quantitative, and think of the qualitative with an implied pejorative, as 'just' perception, or 'just' imagination or 'just' hallucination. Well, Pirsig goes to great lengths to describe the reality of quality, so I come back to my hallucination by the same road."

"Look," Alan said, a little too patiently, "I'm not saying that you didn't actually have an hallucination, or that it wasn't a powerful one. I'm only saying that it was ultimately the sole product of brain cells firing in a certain way in response to your emotions, not the result of divine manipulation."

"Oh, I don't doubt for a minute that my brain cells were firing away, and if such things could be measured they would have shown up on some brain scan somewhere. But what I became convinced of was that my brain cells were the actors in this little drama, but not the author."

Alan started to get a little heated, and said in a heated whisper, "Damnit, pal! You couldn't possibly prove that!"

"Alright, let's try this: you're sitting in the audience watching *Hamlet*. Could you prove right then and there that it was written by Shakespeare?"

"That's ridiculous. We know through experience that the play is fiction, while you're claiming a divine reality. And it would only take a small amount of research to prove convincingly that it was written by Shakespeare."

"Really? Did you know that there exists not a single original autograph of Shakespeare's plays? We only have copies, some made twenty or more years after Shakespeare's death. That's why there are so many theories that people like Thomas Marlow or Sir Francis Bacon actually wrote those plays. So, no: even if you were to leave the theater during intermission and rush out to buy a bound version of the play, it would not be absolute proof that Shakespeare wrote it." Alan was continuing to look more and more annoyed, but I pressed on.

"And yet, regardless of authorship, *Hamlet* has a great deal of meaning in it. Much of it is expressed through tragedy, but clearly it is deep and close

Part II: Dissonance

to the human heart, considering how popular the play has been for over four hundred years. It is a great play, one that we might say has a lot of 'quality,' and that abundance of quality is what also gives the play its abundance of meaning. They are intertwined in an ineffable and mysterious way. So, do I believe that my mom's soul literally crossed a river with a weird looking seafarer, then ascended into light, only to finally run across the beach at Bolinas? Honestly, I don't think that matters very much, just like the fact that the authorship of *Hamlet* has no relevance to its depth of meaning. What matters to both is the meaning conveyed. God can easily author an hallucination and let my brain cells act it out. If I go with the mystery I get a whole lot more than if I belittle it as 'just' an hallucination. In fact, a quote from *Hamlet* is quite apt here:, 'There are more things in Heaven and Earth, Horatio, than are dreamt of in your philosophy.'"

"Well," Alan snorted, "that's just beautiful and poetic and all, but you haven't convinced me that Shakespeare didn't write Hamlet, or that God is producing vignettes in your head. But what's bugging me is not where you are in this story or even who the damn author is, it's how you got into it in the first place."

"Well then enlighten me, O Jedi-master."

"Look, you'd found true love at the same time your mother was dying. Your emotions were all over the place, and at the same time Vivian was convincing you of the reality of the spiritual, mystical world. To please your new love you let yourself get carried away and started fantasizing sea captains and angels."

"Jeez, Alan, haven't you been listening? I was already pretty well convinced of the reality of the spiritual and mystical world."

"Yes, but not in the context of Christianity. Not in this conventional way!" Alan's voice was inching higher. "What is really bothering me is that by being ordained you're taking all of that spirituality and mysticism and tossing it out to become essentially an elected bureaucrat for an organization you've done nothing but complain about for the last nine hundred miles!"

"I haven't . . ."

"One that doesn't seem to have much to do with Zen, or Druids or anything. It seems like your just ceding over your spirituality to what is essentially a religious corporation! That's just crap!"

"First of all, no one, not the followers of Christ, or Yahweh, or Allah or Buddha or Vishnu, cedes over their spiritual selves to the institution. The great masters of all religions and the institutions they left behind are lights

Chapter 8: Nexus I

for the path ahead, but not the path itself. You need to hear the rest of this story, Alan, long as it may be, if you want to understand how I got from here to there, instead of just making assumptions."

"No, I don't. I just don't want to hear it anymore. I've had enough. All you're going to tell me is how Vivian became your religious guide and steered you over the last twenty years to abandon the teachings of your youth, even abandon your visions for Christ's sake, in order to join a conventional religion that she approves of!"

"Wow! Just what are you suggesting?"

Alan was actually shouting by now. "You jerk! I'm not going to use the vulgar term, but let's just say you've been under undue female influence. Can't you see that? You love her and she loves you, but you've become nothing more than a damn follower. I really don't respect organized religion very much anyway, but if you're going to go for it, go for it with integrity, not as some lovesick hanger-on!"

My mouth fell open and I could feel the rush of blood to my head. It was a nasty thing to say, and he knew it the minute the tirade had left his mouth. I was really glad Vivian wasn't in the car, as much for his sake as for hers. But there are some things you just can't take back, and the words hung in the stifled air between us. Alan managed to look shocked, defensive and sullen simultaneously, clearly aware that he had crossed a boundary. But after a few minutes he stubbornly broke the silence.

"I don't think we should talk anymore."

I grunted my agreement, and we sped up Interstate-80 into the cold Wyoming night in silence.

When we finally arrived at the motel in Evanston, I hopped out to go around to Alan's side to help him out, but he was already out and unfolding his white cane. I put an arm on his elbow to help guide him, but he pushed me off, "I can find my own way, even if you can't."

Cane out and tapping, and probably following the Muzak that seeped out through the swinging glass doors, he made his way unsteadily towards the lobby. Trying to navigate an unknown environment, he bumped into a flower pot and a newsstand before finally disappearing through the front doors. I thought as I watched him wobble in just how much it sucked to be blind. But I wondered if he was thinking that I was the one who needed a white cane.

Interlude

I looked back as he smiled, and his words were the whisper of many voices, "Sometimes dreams are wiser than waking."

—GHOST OF THE OLD CHEYENNE TO SHERRIFF
WALT LONGMIRE, *THE COLD DISH*

Chapter 9: The Choke

I FELL ASLEEP FULLY clothed on top of the covers of my queen sized bed in my room at the Evanston Comfort Inn. I had been reading a *Longmire* mystery on my Kindle, but as I dozed it slid off my chest and lay akimbo across the bed. The big difference between Longmire and myself—actually, there are innumerable differences—is that the fictional sheriff of Absaroka County loves Wyoming, and I can't stand it. My prejudice is somewhat justified by years of broken down cars, bad weather and noisy 'sleep optional' motels experienced on many trips back and forth from Colorado to Oregon, and I have never been to the northern parts of the state where Longmire hunts down the bad guys amidst the rugged beauty of the very real Bighorn Mountains. I had only journeyed through the southern part of the state, and the stretch of Interstate-80 between Evanston and Laramie features some of the most butt-ugly scenery you'll find anywhere in the world.

I awoke in the dark, and looked at the clock on the bed stand: 1:23, it blinked. 1:23 . . . 1:23 . . . 1:23 . . . 1:24. I swung my legs over the side of the bed and sat up, spilling the unfortunate Kindle onto the floor, and tried to rub the fog out of my eyes. Thinking I might actually get undressed and go to sleep, I stood up, instantly realizing that sleep had left the building, and might not return that night. Another Wyoming sleep optional motel, though this one was of my own making. So instead of changing, I grabbed a bottled water from the micro-fridge and went to sit out on the micro-porch that adjoined my room. Even through the minimal ambient light of the town, the night sky was a riot of stars and galaxies. Wyoming's southern wastelands are more than made up for by her spectacular night skies, and I

Interlude

settled as best I could into the molded plastic micro-chair and tried to sort out my insomniac thoughts.

The Longmire mysteries take place in the modern—but still wild—west, and like the old west the stories usually feature numerous types of firearms. Old ranchers secret away historic rifles, the bad guys brandish a depressing variety of pistols, and Longmire packs a big .45 Colt. Occasionally a shotgun makes an appearance as what the ranchers refer to as their "varmint guns." Even though a shotgun can be deadly at close range, it seems like they are mostly used to kill rattlesnakes or hunt small game. Since I was not a hunter I was a little fuzzy on the differences between shotguns and rifles, and a quick search on the Internet just before dozing off provided both information and a provocative metaphor for the past day's events.

At the muzzle end of a shotgun barrel is a little part called the choke. It's a little passageway with a smaller diameter than that of the barrel, and its purpose is to compress the little pellets just before they exit the shotgun. Without the choke the pellets would spray all over the place once they left the barrel, but with it the pellets form a much more focused pattern, transforming them from a random and chaotic fate to a purposeful trajectory. A shotgun without a choke is essentially useless except at very close range, but experienced shooters use chokes of different diameters based on the expected range of the target to maximize the effectiveness of their gun.

As a metaphor for focusing human experience I like the choke, even though I don't own a shotgun. There just seem to be times in life when everything gets compressed, emotions run high and a lot of events happen in a short period of time. It hurts. But if you see yourself as a collection of shotgun pellets, then at some point you leave the barrel with the sense that you are flying towards something. Or at least there is some organization to the trajectory you are on. But, just like a lead pellet, you still have no idea of the destination of that trajectory. The shooter who aimed the thing may know, but you don't. And unlike a lead pellet, you can opt out of the trajectory, try flying your own way, and ignore the purposes of the shooter.

I knew when our conversation began that Alan and I would ultimately arrive at this choke point in my own life. Looking backwards I can see a trajectory emerge, but at that time as I began a life with Vivian even as my mother's life ended, I didn't have a clue. But what I didn't expect was Alan's explosive reaction. Usually calm, sarcastic and inquisitive, I knew he nevertheless had the capacity to fly off the handle every now and then. I just couldn't figure out why recounting my vision during my mother's final

Chapter 9: The Choke

moments would set him off like that. It's not as if he had anything at all invested in anything spiritual or religious.

Was it the vision itself that set him off? The ineffable can be very challenging, particularly for people who believe that a scientific and linear explanation must and can be arrived at for all events. If so, then the ambiguity inherent in some modern scientific theories was going to be quite disturbing to an empiricist like Alan. I had read a recent article about the multiverse: the idea that there are an infinite number of universes. In some ways this concept could be used to negate a creative divine component in the universe, since with an infinite number of universes the laws of chance dictate that some universes will support life randomly. On the other hand, the writer of the article could not imagine any way in which the multiverse theory could be proven, given the unimaginably vast expanses of distance and time that would separate these universes, and concluded that scientists might find themselves in the religious position of believing in something they could not prove. They would have to have faith, which might not get them to believe in God but would certainly open the door to other, more divine explanations. Perhaps Alan was feeling the tremendous amount of discomfort a situation like this would cause, or maybe he simply felt that I had thrown in the towel by attaching myself to conventional faith. I wondered if he even imagined that I read articles about the multiverse.

Or was it more personal? Did I represent for him some hope for the integration of the spiritual with the empirical? Had the stories of my unusual upbringing—stories that made me appear in his eyes as a 'Zen-Druid'—misled him into believing I had a different, more exotic trajectory which I was betraying by joining the admittedly prosaic Methodists? Was he right?

The problem was that to get from where we were in my story to where I ended up would require some more story-telling, and I wasn't sure he wanted to listen anymore. I apparently had quickly become a big disappointment. And the problem with the shotgun choke metaphor is that the pellets will ultimately hit something, even if it's not the intended target, which will end both their journey and their purpose; humans, on the other hand, may never know what the target is, and cling to their trajectory in total faith that the shooter knows what he's doing. They might believe that things happen for a reason, even if that reason is not immediately apparent. I'm pretty sure Alan believed that we make our own destiny and that

Interlude

we control our own trajectory. The idea that maybe we don't might be extremely frightening.

Of course, there was one other possibility, and that was that Alan was right. In a few days, I would be ordained into a conventional church institution, and a wilting institution at that. I never had any illusions that I was going to save the Methodist Church, but pursuing a life in ministry produced two fundamental doubts. First, the Methodist Church, or any Protestant church for that matter, didn't really look like a 'Zen-Druid' institution. It proclaimed almost no emphasis on mysticism or meditation, and although intellectually welcoming of a variety of Christian disciplines, in practice it stuck pretty much to a nineteenth century aesthetic of Christianity. Why not, as Alan suggested, pursue a spiritual life that more closely resembled the influences of my upbringing? Why make ministry my career, necessarily cozying up to the institution, when I could make a lot more money in my computer career and still have the time for spiritual pursuits on the side?

The second doubt had also been rather crudely addressed by Alan: was I following someone else's lead? Had I decided to join the ministry to make Vivian happy? This was a tougher nut to crack, since we had become so intertwined over the years. And at first, I had been the one to push ministry as a career even though Vivian had been pursuing spirituality as a vocation for many years. But perhaps the hardest to explain, in spite of all of these doubts, was a deep feeling that what I was doing was right; it was the trajectory I was supposed to be on, no matter how illogical it seemed, and no matter how unable I was to articulate that to Alan, or myself. There was that faith thing again! So, in the car tomorrow, I would tell the rest of the story in the hopes of convincing Alan this was an authentic trajectory. Still, I was pretty certain I would also be trying to convince myself.

With a long series of unanswered questions still swirling around in my head, I decided that sleep would never return to the building unless I did, so I stiffly got up and went back inside. After retrieving the Kindle, I once again lay down on top of the covers and hoped that Longmire would put me back to sleep. It was comforting to read that the fictional county seat of Durant of the fictional Absaroka County had a fictional Methodist church which Longmire's fictional dispatcher attended faithfully. After just a few moments in Longmire's world, the little screen began to blur, and this time I set the Kindle down with a little more dignity and closed my eyes. But they opened again with a start when I heard a soft knocking at my door.

"Hey, buddy. Wake up. Let me in."

Chapter 9: The Choke

The clock now said 3:05 . . . 3:05, and I groggily got up and staggered to the door. Apparently my assessment of a sleepless night had been correct after all. When I opened the door there stood Alan, dressed as I was in the same clothes as yesterday. He apparently suffered from the same insomnia I did, and he brushed past me and into the room, tapping against the walls and bed until he located a chair.

"Well, come on in." I said, closing the door behind him.

Chapter 10: Credo

CLEARLY, ALAN HADN'T SLEPT either. He wasn't one for apologies, but he grumbled at me, "Sorry. It's just that you pissed me off."

"Well, I could see that. What I don't get is what set you off. I opened up to you about a profound and very strange experience, which apparently lit a very short fuse. Is it so important to you that my life be nothing but empirical? That any acknowledgment of the mystical is proof that I'm crazy?"

"No, no. That's not it all. What has frustrated me is that, when I project forward from the life you have so far described for me, I don't see a Methodist minister. It's like you're flushing it all away. I wasn't mad because your experience was stupid; I was mad because your experience was precious."

I had to think about that for a second. "Every thread in my life, and yours too, is precious. These threads make up the weave of your life. If I'm understanding you, what's bothering you is you expected a different quilt to be the result of these threads?"

"What is bothering me, to switch metaphors, is that I don't see any foundation for the life you're choosing now in the life you experienced growing up. It's like you heard a televangelist in the nineties sometime, were born again, halleluiah, and were saved by Jeeeesus."

"So, are you implying that Zen and Druid seem more authentic to you, more real and meaningful, simply because they are exotic?"

Now it was Alan's turn to think for a moment. "Well, actually, yes. Traditional western religion is worn out. Perhaps there was once a great wisdom and power in Jesus Christ and his early followers. But all that's either been beaten away or covered up by centuries of manipulation,

Chapter 10: Credo

misappropriation and misdirection by those whose purpose was only to hijack that power for their own benefit."

"Well, I'm pretty sure you can make the argument that the church over the centuries has had many failings, but I don't think you can make the argument that the message of Jesus has lost its power over the centuries. Its universal appeal often succeeds in spite of the church, to be sure, but the church nevertheless remains the primary method of distribution for the message of the Gospel, and I suspect it has had many, many more quiet successes than it has loud failures. Buddhism and Hinduism and others have had their failings too—look at the San Francisco Zen Center—yet you esteem their message and integrity only because they are less familiar to you. It's the religious version of the grass always being greener in the other temple."

"But do you believe it? Do you actually believe the Christian message? And does that message have enough integrity to overcome the failings of the church?"

"I'll answer your last question first with an emphatic yes! Sometimes we look at all the splits and divisions within the church as a sign of failure, when in fact these splits are often a sign of the Christian path reorganizing itself for a specific people or circumstance because the old ways of the church no longer worked in that context. So, my own understanding of the Christian message may differ in significant ways from others', but that doesn't require one of us to be 'right' and the other one 'wrong.' So, yes, I do actually believe the Christian message as it has come to me and I have received it within the light and context of my own life."

"Alright. So convince me. Show me how you got from point Zen to point Methodist."

"It's four in the morning, Alan, and it's still a pretty long story. Are you sure you want to do this tonight?"

"Then help put me to sleep. Give me the whole journey tomorrow, and just show me the destination tonight. What exactly is it that you believe?"

"Which language do you want me to use? To tell you the truth, I sometimes struggle with conventional Christian language even when describing Christian beliefs."

"Oh please: by all means use your Zen-Druid language!"

I smiled, realizing that Alan may have become fixated on this Zen-Druid thing for a reason. "OK. I believe that there is a Divine Presence in the universe that is distinct from the physical universe that it created. God is as good a word as any for this Divine Presence, but other faiths have other words for a similar concept. For example the Hindi use the term *Brahman* to describe this universal, all enveloping Divine Presence, often described as the Godhead or infinite reality. As I said, this Divinity is distinct from the physical universe, but the physical universe is imbued with its presence. The metaphor I like to use is the tea and the hot water. The tea leaves and the hot water are distinct from each other, but in order to make tea, you must imbue the water with the leaves, and after you do that, it's pretty hard to separate them out again. So it is with the divine and the physical: distinct, but the physical is so imbued with the divine that they appear to be one thing. The mystical element within every human being is a measure of their consciousness of the imbued divine. For Christians, Christ represents the divine, or is the divine really, and so to have a personal relationship with Jesus Christ is a way of acknowledging in an anthropomorphic way this divine presence as real and discernable. I am connected with Christ by sharing this divine presence. I'm also connected to you and all creation by this divine presence.

"But Christ wasn't just another human imbued with the divine presence. He was a singularity—a complete and perfect combination of human and divine—the perfect tea if you want to continue with that metaphor. He was completely conscious of the full extent of his divinity, which he anthropomorphized as The Father, and he was also completely conscious of his humanity, perhaps best epitomized in his tears for the dead Lazarus. But most importantly, he was completely conscious of the combination of the two: a non-differentiation of the tea and the water, if you will. The physical being is so perfectly imbued with the divine that they are no longer distinct: they've formed a new substance. This newness of Christ, so often expounded on in the Gospels, is contagious: each and every one of us can be reborn by borrowing Christ's newness. We still remain imperfect, for we are not Christ, but our newness gives us a vision of perfection that we can live into.

"Living into perfection is not an idea that is exclusive to Christianity. The Hindi, for example, believe that the 'self,' the atman, through the cycle of karma and reincarnation, will eventually meld into the Brahman; a similar idea to the imbuement of the physical nature of creation into the perfection of the divine. What distinguishes Christianity is the concept of resurrection. It is a central element in all Christian faiths and denominations that Christ died—actually died—and then rose from the dead as an enactment of the promise of eternal life."

Chapter 10: Credo

"Don't most Christians say he died as an atonement for sin?"

"Yes, but I'll get to death and atonement in a second. To the skeptical, the resurrection seems impossible, almost silly, and so a matter completely of faith. It seemed that way to me for a long time, and was probably the central stumbling block that kept me from being a Christian for a long time. But if we consider that the physical universe is imbued with the divine—admittedly, also a matter of faith—then we can consider other meanings for the resurrection. Remember I told you way back in Troutdale about a quote I couldn't remember concerning this divine/human relationship that had made me an incarnationalist? Well, I looked it up last night online, and for me, it draws a perfect circle between incarnation and resurrection that is much more satisfying in a physical universe imbued with divinity. It goes:

> Crucifixion wasn't really the hard thing for Jesus. The hard thing was incarnation. Crucifixion and what followed from it—his death and resurrection—were simply the pathway along which infinite consciousness could return to its natural state. What was really hard for infinite consciousness was to come into the finite world in the first place.[1]

"In the resurrection, God returns to being something God always was. If you expressed this incarnationalism in Hindu terms, Brahman became atman—sort of like putting a quart into a pint—but at resurrection, atman reverted to Brahman. God became human for a while, then returned to being God.

"As you mentioned, another aspect of this singularity was the redeeming value of Jesus' death on the cross. Atonement is also a fundamental doctrine of Christianity, and yet it was one that I also had trouble with. Traditional versions are riddled with guilt, assume the foundational nature of sin within humanity, and attract the language of voodoo and magic. And since, two thousand years later, it doesn't appear as if humanity's behavior has changed very much as a result, was it all just an exercise in futility anyway? It's also a doctrine that promotes separateness from God, which I can't really reconcile with a God imbued within creation. If humanity's true and basic nature is sin—a doctrine called original sin—then we must have been created that way, which implies either sinfulness on the part of the creator, or real and insurmountable separateness from a sin-free God. But,

---

1. Bourgeault, *Wisdom Jesus*, 93. Bourgeault is paraphrasing concepts developed by Bernadette Roberts in two of her books: *The Path to No-Self* (1985) and *What is Self?* (2005).

Interlude

the doctrine goes, Christ died so that humanity could be redeemed from all that sin—past, present and future—and thereby reconciled with God. It's as if God made this big boo-boo at the time of creation and has to then pay for it with death. And a temporary death at that. I just don't buy it.

"One thing my Zen background did for me was influence me to seek wholeness rather than separateness, and convince me from a very early age that the basic nature of humanity is good. There is no concept of original sin in Buddhism, and I was never burdened as a child with the assumption that I was fundamentally sinful. Oddly, there really isn't a concept of original sin in in Judaism either. To be sure, in Judaism people sin, but it is in defiance of their true nature, not in compliance with it. Some Christian authors have called this *original blessing*, expressing the idea that long before we sinned, God made us in God's image, blessed us, and called us good. Because, unlike Jesus, we are imperfectly imbued with the divine, we often act against this true nature in actions we call sinful, as a result of free will.

"So, if we accept this idea of original blessing, what is it exactly that Jesus is atoning for on behalf of humanity? And if Jesus is the perfect embodiment of the Divine, to whom exactly is this ransom paid? A ransom paid to one's self is not a ransom. If that ransom is death, then it's simply suicide. Keep in mind, Alan: for ideas like these I would have been burned at the stake as a heretic in times past, but Christians attach so much importance to the atonement of Christ that I really wanted to find a way to understand it that didn't include ransoms, blood payments or suicide. Since I am an incarnationalist, let's look at it through that lens.

"According to Paul's letter to the church in Philippi, God emptied himself of his Godness in order to incarnate as a human and be obedient to God's own laws, including death on a cross. So, to un-anthropomorphize this statement—good lord, is there really such a word?—the universal Divine squeezed itself into human form. Normally you can't really put a quart into a pint, but nevertheless no attributes of the Divine were left behind in the process. Just like a single strand of DNA contains everything about an individual, Jesus can be fully divine and fully human. You might say that he, paradoxically, had complete human DNA and complete divine DNA, perfectly meshed. So, we have a man who can weep for Lazarus and still restore his life. At Jesus' death, the human body is left behind, and the divine restored to its divine stature: *infinite consciousness returning to infinite consciousness*. But more than knowledge was gained by this little divine side-trip, and it wasn't just curiosity that led the Divine on this adventure.

Chapter 10: Credo

Becoming human has consequences even for the Divine. God felt the lash of the whip, the weight of the cross and the stab of the nails through the skin of Christ. The thorns tore his brow as he tasted the vinegar. Christ did not endure this torture and sacrifice himself as a masochistic blood-tribute for sin; through experiencing the bitter dregs of sin God, who is also *infinite love*, altered human spiritual DNA so that we can no longer claim ignorance of God's presence. The divine presence changed the hot water so that it could become fully aware of the tea. We have been given an unmistakable call to seek the same human/divine perfection that was evident in Jesus, and we have been given the means to answer that call. Jesus called this the 'new covenant in my blood'[2] during the institution of the Lord's Supper. In dying on the cross, the relationship between creator and created was changed. The atonement was not a transaction, it was this new covenant Jesus spoke of: *I will show you the path; you must follow it. The divine presence will catch you if you stumble, but if you consistently wander off deliberately, you might find yourself on your own. Creating separateness from God is the foundation of sin.* We are freed from sin in the sense that we no longer have any excuses. Or, in a more Zen-like formulation, seeking wholeness with the divine is the lighted path; you can only hide from God alone in the dark."

The furrows in Alan's brow had been getting deeper and deeper as I pushed my way through this. Finally, he characteristically sought refuge in a wise-crack. "I liked the guilt better. It was a lot easier."

"The Christian path encourages us to seek that original blessing within ourselves, rather than wallow in guilt over ingrown sin. We are imbued with the Divine, and since the Divine was changed by the Christ experience, so too must we be inevitably changed."

"But how can God change? I thought he was omniscient and he knows everything through all of time."

"Omniscient is a human term, describing something that humans can imagine. The Divine is not limited by human consciousness and exists in a way we cannot imagine, even if we can experience it. Under that rubric, there's no reason at all that infinite consciousness couldn't change while simultaneously knowing everything. After all, what is 'knowing' to God?"

Alan's brow remained furrowed, but he admitted, "I guess I'm starting to see the picture. You're trying to reconcile specifically Christian beliefs with universal spiritual concepts. How can you do that? I mean, Christians

---

2. Luke 22:20 (NIV)

are famous for classifying people as 'saved' or 'unsaved,' and you damn well better be a Christian if you want to be in the saved category. Can't you see that this is a fundamental problem? That by becoming a Christian, in spite of all your Zen-Druid language, you're basically condemning all of your early spiritual experiences to hell!"

There it was. We'd finally come to it. "That's what's really bugging you, isn't it? That's why you blew up at me after I shared the experience of my mother's death with you?"

Alan looked a little chagrined, but he wasn't backing down. "Well, yeah, that's most of it. I listened for two days to these weird and marvelous experiences you've had, but when I put them up against the choices you've made recently, I'm sorry: I saw a hypocrite. It's like all of your past frightens you, and you've reduced yourself in order to take safe harbor in conventionality."

"Well . . . You've really made a lot of assumptions, Alan, one of them being that my path got narrower rather than broader as I more fully embraced Christianity. Let's start with the first incorrect assumption: that I have embraced what is called 'Christian Exclusivity,' the idea that only Christians can be fully involved with the Divine Presence and therefore are the only people that God will 'save.' While Christians rest in heaven for eternity, everybody else burns in hell; that's the picture you're thinking of, right? It is true, there are many Christians who believe this, literally interpreting several passages in the Gospels that indicate only believers in Christ will be rewarded by The Father, while everyone else goes into the outer darkness with wailing and gnashing of teeth. Individual Christian denominations over the centuries have become convinced that they alone have the magic combination of beliefs for salvation, not just in comparison to other religions but to other Christians as well. Wars have been fought over things like that.

"Christian Exclusivity is hard to defend if you believe in the universality of Christ's atonement. And it brings with it the worst of both worlds. On the one hand, you're effectively denying that God's grace exists for much of the world's population, and no matter how good, generous, decent and giving an individual like, say, Shinryu Suzuki was, he is now and for eternity immersed in a lake of fire. I came to see that believing you have exclusive knowledge of how God's grace functions in the world is proof that you don't. And secondly—and I think this is a point many people miss—believing that you are a member of an exclusive club retards your ability to be

Chapter 10: Credo

fully Christian. It focuses you on static beliefs and away from the active path. After all, why bother to seek the Divine Presence if you think you've already found it? It's the old, false, Calvinistic belief that if you're elected for salvation, you're elected and there's nothing positive or negative you can do about it."

"Wait, wait. Isn't that what Grandpa Arminius objected to, way back in Portland?"

"No, not my great-grandpa, but yes, Jacobus Arminius the Dutch reformer objected to unconditional election and double predestination, which is basically, and definitively: if you're in, you're in, and if you're out, you're out. He believed that there simply was no room for grace in that formula, and who was he or any other human to put limits on God's grace? And now that I think about it, Arminius also contributed to my first point, in that he also rejected the idea of limited atonement, which is the idea that the atoning power of Christ's death only applies to those who are already elected. No, no, NO! The new covenant made at Christ's death was with humanity—all humanity—not a particular subset."

"OK, OK, keep your voice down. Does the Bible back you up on this?"

I lowered it down a notch, but kept going. "Well, look at the story of the Three Wise Men in the Gospel of Matthew. They're Gentiles: they're not Jewish, and are usually thought of as Persians. Among other things, they represent the revelation of God in Christ to the Gentiles, a vast and rather non-exclusive club. Even at his birth, God is revealed in Christ to the whole of humanity, not just a subset. And other stories, like the Syro-Phoenician woman, where Jesus heals the daughter of a non-Jew based solely on her great faith, makes the same point. I think the Bible supports the idea of universal atonement—the universal availability of God's grace—very well. So, if the Christ experience is universal, how can Christians claim it only for themselves?

"This is exactly the depth that is missed by claiming Christian Exclusivity. Instead of looking for connections, you're looking for disconnections. Instead of looking for wholeness, you're looking for separateness. Instead of seeking the Way of Christ, you're stuck with monolithic beliefs. And instead of seeking grace, you're really just seeking the power of self-justification. Or to put it in the simplest possible way, you've stopped seeking God."

Alan kept poking: "But doesn't all that lead to unconsidered pluralism? I mean, if everything is true, or at least equal, then nothing has value.

Interlude

What difference does it make if I'm a Christian, or a Jew, or a Muslim, if all that matters is I have equal access to this Divine Presence?"

"Well, that's another common mistake. Let's use the well-trod journey metaphor one more time to try and straighten that one out. Pluralism tends to suggest exactly what you just said, that all paths are equally valid; but for some reason this has led people to believe that in order to be accepting of other paths, they have to water down their own beliefs in order to find some lowest common denominator. You have to dumb your own path down in order to get it on the same plane with others. Why? The best way to be a tolerant Christian is to embrace the Christian path fully. Love God with all your heart, mind and soul; love your neighbor; grow in wisdom; spend more time in prayer today than you did yesterday. Accept the gift of the new covenant in the atonement and live by the precepts of peace and harmony that Jesus taught. Do you really have to condemn the Hindu or the Muslim in order to do that? Must *you* be the one to control all the paths that God has laid out? Could you? Must *you* limit Christ's atonement? Could you? No, of course not all paths are equal, simply because free will can cause any of us to stumble and stray into the weeds, taking others with us who are easily swayed. But why not seek the highest common denominator? It's OK to examine other paths and find those points of connectedness, but it's also important to recognize areas of significant variance: we might struggle to find denominators, high or low. However, if we assume that all other paths are just absolutely and intrinsically wrong, we make a big and unjustifiable assumption about the nature of God and God's grace. Trying to define and confine God because of our own limited vision simply confines ourselves; so just thank God every day for the clarity of your own path, and pray that others find the same clarity on theirs."

Alan tried to get a word in edgewise, but I pressed on. "Or, here's another way to look at it. There are substantive differences between what Luther believed in and what was espoused later by the Lutherans. The beliefs of Calvin and the Calvinists don't completely correspond. You can actually make the same differentiation between who Christ *is* and what Christians *are*. As an embodiment of the Divine Presence, as *infinite consciousness*, Christ is not confined to Christianity. So, it would be untrue to say that all Buddhists or Muslims are really Christians under the hood: that's untrue and offensive, actually. But it *is* true that all humans share the imbued Divine Presence that Christ once embodied. That's what, to return to conventional Christian language, 'He died for all' means. When Jesus says, 'you

Chapter 10: Credo

must believe in me' he means in order to participate with the Divine Presence you must accept the reality of the Divine Presence, not that you must be a Jew as he was, or that you must now be a Christian. The covenant isn't between the Divine Presence and Christians only, it is between the Divine Presence and humanity."

Again Alan opened his mouth to speak, but then popped it shut as he sat and tried to absorb all of this. I frankly was a little out of steam at 4 a.m. and let the silence settle over us like a soft blanket. After the fight in the car and Alan's inbred cynicism, I was holding my breath in suspense over his reaction to my musings. Finally, he stirred a little and said, "What was it you called that guy, Alan Watts? Some Buddhist word thing?"

"Uh . . . you mean what Suzuki-roshi called him? A bodhisattva?"

"That's it. A bodhisattva. From now on, I'm going to stop calling you a Zen-Druid. What you really are is a Christian bodhisattva!"

I burst out laughing. "Holy cow! Houston, the Eagle has landed!" We both laughed uproariously, no longer caring if we woke the neighbors. Somehow we had latched upon a term for my peculiar brand of metaphysics that satisfied Alan, even if it was completely inaccurate. At 4 a.m. you take what you can get. The tension between us evaporated as our laughter dwindled down to giggles, then snuffles, then silence.

Finally, Alan stood up, and said rather stiffly, "OK, you have answered satisfactorily my concerns about the spiritual life. I don't share your views, but at last I think I understand your views. You have connected Zen and Christianity, east and west for me, and so in that way I can tell you have not sliced off your past completely from your present." He paused at the door, then said, "But you're not off the hook yet. While I respect your spiritual views, I have a real loathing for the church. The two don't seem connected to me at all. I'll be interested to see if you can be as convincing, or as convicted, about the church you're about to get into bed with."

"Good night, Alan."

"Good night, Pastor-roshi." Alan slipped out the door, tapping his cane against the wall.

I went and lay down on the bed, and sleep finally began to bear down on me relentlessly. But before fully succumbing, I fleetingly fretted about what the next day's conversations would bring. In spite of having cleared the air on spirituality, Alan had homed right in on the one area I knew I was less certain about. Yes, we had passed through the choke and were now on a fixed trajectory; two tightly bound pellets aimed at—what? We had gotten

Interlude

through my—what?—but I still had no idea what Alan's—what?— was. As sleep overtook me, I hoped that wherever the shooter had aimed us, we weren't travelling rapidly towards a rattlesnake.

Part III: Counterpoint

You look at where you're going and where you are and it never makes sense, but then you look back at where you've been and a pattern seems to emerge.
—ROBERT M. PIRSIG, *ZEN AND THE ART OF MOTORCYCLE MAINTENANCE*

Chapter 11: Passages

I AWOKE WITH A start and after a few foggy moments realized my cell phone was ringing in my pocket. It was Vivian. "Where are you? Are you alright?" I looked around disoriented, until I finally recognized the darkened parking lot of the Safeway in Conifer. I'd never even gone inside and really couldn't remember why I'd driven all the way down there.

"We've had dinner and got home and you weren't here! Hello? Is everything OK?"

"Yeah, yeah. OK," I mumbled. "Just heading home now . . . Uh, fell asleep . . ."

I started the car and, devoid of groceries, wound my way back onto 285, heading south again to Bailey, but I couldn't help but think of all that I had not told Alan. In particular, all of the closed doors, all of the unconsidered decisions and blind luck that had steered my life. I had left him in that motel in Evanston with the impression that I had arrived at a statement of faith after integrating my upbringing with some of the harsher realities of adulthood. It just wasn't that simple. It's never that simple. The truth was, in 1985 I could never had made that statement to Alan or anyone else, but the process by which I could arrive at such a statement still seemed foggy to me, involving lots of subconscious work over the subsequent twenty years. More than Alan, I needed to understand that process before Saturday. I wanted to be ordained whole, and not in pieces.

The sun had gone to bed hours ago by the time I got back to the cabin, but the moon was wide awake on an unusually warm June night. Vivian fussed at me for a few moments when I came in, understandably so considering my long absence, but by now my brain was racing with memories

Part III: Counterpoint

and anxieties. After a little while, she moved to the sofa and began reading from her Kindle, and I retreated to the back porch to enjoy the moon and stars for a few minutes. I settled into the peace and quiet, and was inevitably drawn back to the journey.

Alan and I pulled out of the Comfort Inn just before 9 a.m., and coasted down the main drag to the interstate. God must have heard my moaning about Wyoming the night before and was trying his hardest to change my opinion. In the Rockies, June isn't early summer, it's mid-spring, and as we swung out on to the freeway the wild flowers in the unkempt strips by the road were still trying to push up through the grass and grab some of the brilliant-cold early morning sun. Alan looked wan and pale, no doubt a result of too little sleep, but he put his aviator dark glasses back on and rolled down the window to let his elbow out into the cool air. Nobody was going to mistake us for a couple of Wyoming cowboys, but I began to feel more forgiving towards the state.

Alan found the radio knob and began scanning through the local AM stations: country & western (whrrr, static), country and western (whrrr, static), country and western (whrrr, static), Rush Limbaugh (whrrr, static), country and western (whrrr, static), Mexican (whrrr, static), country and . . . Alan fumbled for the on/off switch and returned us to silent meditation. Each of us had gotten maybe three or four hours of sleep, packed up and picked at the detritus of the "Free Continental Breakfast!" before stumbling into the car. In spite of the struggling beauty in and around Evanston, I suspected being half asleep might be the best way to get through southern Wyoming.

"So, do you still think I'm a Christian bodhisattva?"

Alan yawned. "Frankly, I'm still not totally sure what a bodhisattva is, but nevertheless, you are one."

Clunk. That conversation petered out faster than it had begun. We were now fully on to the freeway, and the greener pastures of Evanston were rapidly being replaced with the grey and brown sand and tumbleweed that passed for scenery in this part of the country. Alan took his turn to try and start the conversation. "You've been through here a lot, right?"

Chapter 11: Passages

"Vivian and I used to drive through here a couple of times every year when we lived in Colorado Springs and her parents lived up on the Washington coast."

"How on earth did you, Mr. Zen-Druid-Guitarist-California-boy-Christian Bodhisattva, end up in Colorado Springs?"

"It has a lot to do with my love/hate relationship with the Northwest..."

"Like your love/hate relationship with Wyoming?"

"Pretty much. I usually just drive through Wyoming, but I had to live in the Northwest. You realize, don't you, that you're asking me to relate some more life-history, which you recently called 'ridiculous.'"

"Well, I guess your life history is slightly less boring than a blind guy driving through southern Wyoming, so I relent: let's hear your banal story as the miles fly by!"

Alan seemed to have recovered himself, so I plowed ahead. "Well, you were right about one thing: the rest of this story is all pretty much wrapped around Vivian, including ending up in Colorado Springs. After my divorce from Pamela was finalized, we got married in 1985 at a beautiful little Congregational church in Murphys, where we had held Mom's services just a few months before." I laughed a little. "My sister was in attendance along with her five year old son, Joshua. Joshua had apparently decided that he was the one who was going to marry Vivian, and when he found out it was his Uncle John who had won the prize, he was furious. We asked him to ring the church bell at the beginning of the ceremony, which he did, but then he returned to his pew stomping his feet with such dramatic flair that everybody laughed while he pouted through the rest of the ceremony. It was a lovely small wedding that everybody enjoyed; except Joshua, of course.

"After we got married we thought our lives were going in one direction, when in fact they were going in another. The illusory path was that we were going to be professional singers, and we both threw ourselves into our lessons and coaching, performing frequently in local Gilbert & Sullivan productions and occasionally in a local opera production. We supported ourselves with temp jobs and office jobs, and I began working more regularly in the computer industry. The plan was these would keep body and soul together until we got our big break in music. Well, Man plans and God laughs. Vivian got pregnant a few weeks after we were married..."

"You rascal!"

"... and our oldest boy Jonathan was born the next February. By the time Jeffrey came along two years later..."

Part III: Counterpoint

"You laggard!"

"Jeez, ALAN! By the time Jeffrey came along two years later, it was beginning to dawn on us that the Bay Area was becoming a lousy and very expensive place to raise kids. On top of that, it seemed clear our big musical break wasn't coming, and I was starting to get successful at my computer jobs. When a friend of ours who was also trying to make a career in opera said, 'They don't pay you to sing, they pay you to travel,' we realized that our desire for family was not compatible with our desire for music careers, and we began to cast about for something different. In June of 1989 I did a phone interview with a utility district in Everett, Washington, and much to my surprise was offered the job. I convinced myself that the rain in Washington wasn't all that bad—and somehow convinced Vivian too—so I accepted the job and we prepared to move."

"OK, stop for a sec." Alan said peevishly. "You've spent the last two days describing a spiritual journey: the Zen thing, the music thing, the nature thing. Did all of this come to a screeching halt when you got married and had kids?"

"Screeching? No. But they all morphed into something different. This period between my mother dying and our moving to Snohomish in 1989 was sort of like merging from one busy freeway onto another. Like I said, one trajectory to another. One moment you're on I-5 heading to Portland, and without realizing it you've merged onto I-84 and are heading for Colorado."

"You might want to hunt for something other than freeway metaphors . . ."

"Sorry, but it can happen so slowly you don't know that it's happening at all, yet you wake up one day and find yourself on a completely different road. Hmm . . . find yourself . . . What hasn't changed, he said stubbornly sticking to a travel metaphor, is that you're still carrying the same baggage.

"The 'Zen thing' had pretty much petered out before Mom died. I still carried my admiration and respect for Suzuki-roshi, as I do to this day, but Mom had detached herself from the 'Zen thing' and so I had no active or even passive involvement with Zen. Vivian was interested in Christian contemplative practices, but back in those days that was her thing. I was pretty much focused in on having a career, and Christianity had only grown from an irrelevance to a curiosity, but not much more than that. And with no real possibility for a music career, that too turned into a hobby, albeit mostly practiced in church settings.

Chapter 11: Passages

"The 'nature thing' ended up leaving a huge hole in my heart, one that has only recently been filled. After mom died and Vivian and I got married, we spent more and more time in career pursuit and less and less time at Pinecrest. Dad was still living in Murphys and Pinecrest held less relevance for him as well. He also was actively losing his battle with alcoholism to the point where I had to forbid him from seeing my two kids. Still, there were a couple of magical moments left at the cabin. Vivian and I honeymooned there, and I brought my oldest boy Jonathan there a few times to wade in the lake and take boat rides.

"On the day after Christmas in 1988 I received a call from a young man who had been renting a room at Dad's house: Dad had died. It was and remains a strange, bittersweet feeling. Dad had had heart problems for several years, including a major heart attack a few years before, and although he technically died of heart failure, he had been on a committed program of suicide by alcohol for a long time. And he just sort of snuck out of my life. By the time we got to Murphys the next day, his body had already been cremated, leaving me with a profound sense of the incompleteness of our relationship. You have things that you want and expect from your parents, from your dad, and if you don't get them before they die you can never get them. It creates guilt and regret, and becomes the ultimate driver of adult children of alcoholics symptoms.

"We held Dad's funeral in the same Congregational church in Murphys where we had held Mom's, and where Vivian and I had gotten married. It was surprisingly well attended, and it made me realize that not everyone shared my ambivalence towards my Dad. One family friend, who had witnessed some of Dad's worst alcoholic episodes, spoke of him like a second father. I remember thinking bitterly at the time that I wished he had been a first father.

"Still, one result of Dad's death was that none of his four kids had the wherewithal to afford the upkeep on the cabin, and we decided we would need to sell it. That's the huge hole I was talking about. Attachment to place only works if you can keep the place. The cabin, as tumble-down as it was, sold quickly and for more than our asking price, and escrow closed early in July, 1989. My oldest brother Norm was Dad's executor and handled most of the details but, just as I had been handed the task of putting our dog to sleep so many years before, I was also handed the task of closing down the cabin for the last time. I took three year old Jonathan with me and we made the familiar drive across the Central Valley together one last time. Most of the fruit stands were gone by then, replaced by rubber-stamp homes in huge suburban tracts for long distance commuters into Silicon Valley. But the A&W Root Beer stand was still there in Oakdale and I couldn't resist giving Jonathan a little treat. When we arrived at the lake we had to hike in to the cabin, since we had already sold our boat. The cabin was indeed forlorn when we arrived there.

"Jonathan and I spent the night, then the next morning we set about the melancholy task of closing the cabin down one last time. We had already removed our personal belongings, but left behind the worn out deck furniture, beds and miscellaneous bureaus and chairs. I set about doing the normal things like shutting off the water, locking the bathroom, closing the shutters, and finally locking the kitchen door behind me. I sat Jonathan down on the picnic table and took one last look around, and began to sob. Everything I told you about Pinecrest, Alan, was just a sampler of all the vivid experiences I had had by the lake. It was like watching a movie where a boat unexpectedly sinks; for a moment I felt like the drowning man watching the rescue ship sail away over the horizon. Mom was gone, Dad was gone, and this, my only other anchor to the past, was now gone too, sold to the highest bidder. If you haven't already figured it out I can be quite dramatic as the occasion arises, and for a moment thought I might slip into the same darkness that had overcome me years before in Los Altos. Jonathan, God bless his soul, became quite upset to see his Dad crying, and finally told me what we had always told him when he was upset: 'Daddy, you be a happy boy now!'

"From our children we learn to embrace the future. After a few more sniffles, I hoisted Jonathan up on my shoulders and we headed back down the trail without once looking back. We returned to our home in the Bay Area, and in a few days I left to start my new job in Washington. Vivian and the boys followed a few weeks later. We found a nice house in Snohomish and believed we were settling down to a conventional middle class life."

Alan honored my reverie for as long as he could, but finally jumped in, "You claimed earlier that you were on a trajectory that would connect your Zen-Druid past to your Methodist future. I guess there's more to come, but as of now I'm not seeing it. I'm seeing a guy who got on a path similar to mine; similar to the path you and I seemed to share. All of this trajectory talk and yet you seemed to be shooting off into suburban obscurity."

I shook my head, although Alan couldn't see it. "And as I have said before, the path you're on may appear to be headed in a certain direction,

Chapter 11: Passages

when in fact the destination is quite unexpected. And it's a destination you could only have reached by being on that path. Just because a direction seems inevitable in hindsight doesn't make it so at the time. I tend to think of those years as a fallow time, when great growth is going on, but it's all underground.

"As much as I enjoyed being a husband and father, and the suburban middle-class lifestyle, I was disturbed by the sense that what I was doing then had nothing to do with what I had been doing before. I felt like my life had been bisected. I had no friends remaining from my childhood, no parents to keep in touch with, barely in touch with my own siblings. The cabin was gone and I had moved to a different state. The feeling was exactly what you have been describing: the sense that the first part of my life had nothing to do with the second part of my life."

"Well, were you even participating in any religious activities, or had that gone fallow too?"

"I continued working as a music and choir director in Everett, and combined with Vivian's desire to bring up our kids with a religious foundation, I spent most every Sunday in church."

"Is this where you finally admit to me that you got suckered into conventional religion, and that the church wooed you magically into giving up being a Zen-Druid?"

"Hardly. To hear these stories, you would think I would have gone running back to the woods. But it's complicated."

"Of course it is . . ."

Chapter 12: The Guilt List

How do you describe a fallow time? So much is happening, all of it hidden. On the surface, there was lots of motion in my life during these years, but all of the progress was hidden. This is what gave me the sense of being on one trajectory when in fact I was on another. The irony of reliving these memories while driving through the barren lands of southern Wyoming was not lost on me. The land there seems permanently fallow. The surface supports only hardy grasses and tumbleweeds, while the riches of the land, the minerals and the oil, lie far beneath the surface. The casual traveler would dismiss the area as a wasteland, never realizing the treasures beneath their feet. I in fact had driven over these treasures many times, but only now realized how the barrenness is so necessary to support them. Once again I emerged from reverie to try and engage with Alan.

"Driving along this route brings back a lot of memories."

"Any of them good?"

"Well, some were pretty annoying at the time, but make for funny stories now."

"Like what?"

"One time Vivian and I and the kids were travelling through Wyoming in the middle of winter. We were going to visit Vivian's parents for Christmas, and they lived out on the coast of Washington. It was snowing like crazy and colder than hell, but we made it to the motel in Rawlins where we had reservations. When I checked in, I asked the clerk to put in a 6 a.m. wakeup call to our room. No problem. We unpacked, and went to bed. I was awakened by the wake-up call on the phone, got up and dressed, and took the dog for a walk. It was the middle of winter, so it would still be dark

Chapter 12: The Guilt List

out at 6 a.m. and I didn't think anything of it. The problem was, when I got back to the room and looked at the clock, it was 2:20 a.m. The clerk had sent in the wake up call, all right, but at 2 a.m.! Not too funny at the time, but the real laugh came a year later, when we repeated the trip from Colorado Springs to Washington, and pulled up at a hotel in Rawlins, and low and behold: I had booked us inadvertently into the same hotel! Needless to say, we didn't leave a wakeup call, and for all future trips we made sure to stay in Evanston. Out of all this was born the myth of the 'sleep optional' motel."

"I'll bet they didn't even have a 'Free Continental Breakfast!'"

"They did not."

"Well, anyway, we left your ridiculous life-history just as you and Vivian were moving to Washington State, a journey that does not require a trip through Wyoming. How'd you get from there to Colorado?"

"As I said, we moved to Snohomish, Washington, just north of Seattle in 1989. This really marked the beginning of my flight into illusory middle-class security. I took a programming job at a Public Utility District, bought a nice daylight rambler a ways out into the country, and focused on making money and raising kids. That's what I did from 1989 to 2006, first in Washington, then in Colorado Springs, then in Forest Grove, Oregon. And, before you even ask, I didn't, and don't regret this at all, particularly when I recall all of the great times I had in raising my two boys. Disneyland, Cub Scouts, the whole nine yards. But at the time, I thought *this is it*. I couldn't see that period of my life as the middle part of a longer journey and so suffered that peculiar anxiety of encroaching middle age. And in terms of spiritual growth . . . I don't know. Actually, quite a number of things happened during these years, but in retrospect one thing really stands out to me: after being so critical of my Dad and the way he got Peter-Principled into alcoholism and unhappiness, there I was firmly on the same path. The difference is, I got motivated to consciously pull away from that. I don't know why Dad couldn't, or wouldn't, but he didn't. He really liked working for a cutting edge engineering company when he first started out, just like I did thirty years later, and he liked science and was actually a pretty smart guy. But I got the impression he was emotionally compromised even as a child, and perhaps that left him short on resources to fight his addictive behavior. But I felt a lot more sympathy for him after I had been in the corporate world for a while than I had as a child. I liked working as a programmer, using cutting edge PC programming tools and languages, and I had a knack for it. But you learn after a while that there is a difference between liking what you do and seeking meaning in what you do. And as these fallow years went by I could more clearly see how Dad had gotten seduced by the security of his job, to the abandonment of his spirit.

"The same might have happened to me had we stayed in Snohomish. I liked working for the PUD. I liked being part of a group that, when a big storm would hit, would do all sorts of heroic things out in the wind and rain to get power restored. They, of course, were the linemen, not the programmers, but still . . . One time, when the Snohomish River flooded, one of these guys put on scuba gear and dove into the flooded Weyerhaeuser mill to shut off the electricity ten feet under water. Yikes! We had a nice house outside of town, and our kids were at a good private school. Vivian and I even started a little community theater company. I conducted the orchestra, Vivian produced and directed. It was a full and interesting life."

"Well, for goodness sake! Why did you leave?"

"Two reasons, really. The primary one was that the weather was atrocious. Our house there was in what they called a *convergent zone*, a fact the real estate agent hadn't mentioned when we bought it. Storms coming in over the Cascades to the east and storms coming in from Puget Sound to the west would converge precisely above our house, making it pretty much the rainiest part of the rainiest state. I managed OK, but Vivian spent a lot of time trapped at home with two little kids, and after five years she had kinda had it. Actually, she had really had it. She suffered from Seasonal Affective Disorder, and really struggled when there was no sunshine and constant drizzle for weeks on end. I think it really came home to her one year when the Fourth of July fireworks celebration was rained out. We tried those little lights you can get, we tried getting away more, but in the end there was nothing for it: we had to move to a sunnier climate.

"The second reason had to do with the fun not being the same as the meaningful. At the time I just thought I had a restless soul and was thus compelled to move on after a certain amount of time. But now I wonder if I was unconsciously feeling like I was just treading water. The break that came in 1989 had been a big break. I had moved away from California where I had lived all of my life, we had sold Pinecrest, my Mom and Dad were gone, and I had given up on a music career. All of those things I was blabbing about from Portland to Evanston were fading into the past, and I had this nagging feeling that there was a hole in my life; that I had become disconnected from all of those things that were important and memorable about my childhood. But I was pretty schizophrenic about it, in the sense

Chapter 12: The Guilt List

that I was seeking connectedness while running away from it at the same time. For example, my sister had divorced her husband and moved up to Snohomish to be closer to Vivian and me. My response: within a year we moved away. That was a major entry on my guilt list for many years."

I wallowed for a few moments in silence, and for once Alan kept his mouth shut.

"Well, anyway," I resumed, "I put my resume out with headhunters and was surprised when I got a call from MCI in Colorado Springs asking for a phone interview. I'd never been to Colorado in my life, but when we received a booklet from the Colorado Springs Chamber of Commerce stating that the Springs had more than three hundred days a year when the sun shined, Vivian said, 'You're taking that job!'

"I rented a small U-Haul and drove, for the first of many times, along this very same route. I stayed in that same motel in Evanston on New Year's Eve, 1994, when I got my first taste of sub-zero weather. I had never experienced a frozen moustache before, and the next morning I ate the first of many 'Free Continental Breakfasts.' I arrived for the very first time in Colorado on New Year's Day, 1995, and stayed with my Aunt Maggie and Uncle Bill in Monument for a month or so until Vivian sold the house in Snohomish and moved out with the boys in late February."

"The same Aunt Maggie and Uncle Bill who were at Pinecrest?" I nodded. "So you ran away from connectedness by running towards connectedness with your family?"

"You know, in some ways I was like an addict. I craved connectedness with my past and my family, but I wanted to avoid it at the same time. Very weird. That's why this whole story is like a Ping-Pong match, back and forth, back and forth. For the 4 ½ years we lived in Colorado Springs, we saw Bill and Maggie maybe once a year, even though we lived within ten miles. So that went onto my guilt list too. Can you think of anything more useless than a guilt list?"

"You're not going to wallow again, are you? It sounds like you were pretty confused, not unlike a lot of people as middle-age approaches."

"The funny thing is, Colorado Springs was in many ways better than Snohomish on the family front. Practically the day we moved in we instantly fell in love with Colorado. The boys were Cub Scout age, and we took many Cub Scout and family camping trips into the Rockies. Our house had a clear view of Pike's Peak from the back porch, and we had a nice house in a safe neighborhood. The only drawback was my job with MCI demanded a lot of my time, and I had to travel a lot.

"For me, though, and for my soul and happiness, I felt like I had my mountains back again. The Rockies are different from the gentler Sierras, but I couldn't help but resonate with the forests and lakes that partially filled the void left by the loss of Pinecrest. If you can't be with the one you love . . ."

Alan grimaced. "I don't think we're gonna find Steve Stills on the radio out here but, hey, that was a pretty awful imitation."

"Thanks. On Saturdays in the fall, there would be football games at the Air Force Academy, which was just a couple miles north of our house. Being the Air Force they often would have fly-overs before the game, and the planes would circle right above our neighborhood, waiting for their cue to zoom over the stadium. The boys and I would get stiff necks looking up, watching the planes circle overhead. It's memories like that that you cherish. Vivian loved the town, loved the mountains, and Vivian also began some serious spirituality training at a convent in the middle of Colorado Springs.

"But fate again intervened. MCI was purchased by WorldCom, and they decided to sell all the programmers to EDI as contractors. I really didn't want to work for Ross Perot, so I started casting about for a different job. At the same time, Vivian's parents came to visit with us, and it was sadly and painfully obvious that they couldn't handle the altitude: at 6,200 feet Colorado Springs is in the 'lowlands' of Colorado. So we were also faced with the dilemma of aging parents who were far away and wouldn't be able to see their grandchildren very often.

"Finally, in the summer of 1999, I got an invitation for an interview with a dot-com in Portland. I flew up there and went to the interview, but I must say I have never had an interview go worse. I fumbled and stumbled and gave answers that were painfully wrong, and I walked out of there knowing there was no way I was going to get that job. I remember sitting in the Portland airport waiting for my flight back to Colorado and having this powerful wave of relief come over me. We would stay in Colorado Springs, I thought, and I'd find another job or just go ahead and work for EDI. I've rarely had such a strong feeling of inevitability come over me, and I have never been so wrong.

"When I got back to Colorado Springs, the dot-com had already called and offered me the job. I gallantly told Vivian how I had a message from God in the Portland airport telling me to not take the job, and that we'd stay

Chapter 12: The Guilt List

and work things out in Colorado. But it just wasn't that simple. I had forgotten about the kids having access to their grandparents, and I had been certain that I would not get the job in Portland. I began to realize it probably wasn't the voice of God that had spoken to me in the Portland airport, and that there are times in life when you simply have to make choices based on duty rather than personal desires. Vivian, being the smart one, had pretty much worked all of this through by the time I came home, and she too was dubious of God's voice in my ear at the Portland airport. So, in the end, we packed everything up and moved to Forest Grove, Oregon, about thirty miles west of Portland."

"Was it the right decision?"

I was quiet for so long that Alan asked nervously, "Hey, are you awake over there? Is anyone driving the car?"

"Sorry. I remember when we told Bill and Maggie we were moving away to take care of Vivian's parents, Maggie asked plaintively, 'Who's going to take care of us?' Another entry on the guilt list . . . But, to answer your question more directly, let's see . . . The dot-com job in Portland turned out to be awful and ended up being the only job I was ever laid off from; Vivian's parents didn't really want our help so that got to be very uncomfortable; the kids had a lot of trouble adjusting to the new area . . . On the other hand, I eventually got a good paying job with GE Medical Systems, and after a while the distinction between 'enjoying' and 'meaningful' began to get clearer. In other words, the trajectory became less ambiguous. Let's just say that when you are swimming through shark infested waters and someone asks you 'is it worth it,' you might hesitate. But when you reach dry ground and your wounds are healing, you realize there was no other way to get there."

"Wow! Shark infested waters! Healing wounds! So, Dr. Jones, is this going to get all melodramatic again?"

I bit my lip, once again wondering about the wisdom of opening up sensitive memories to Alan's sarcasm. But, we'd come this far, so, once more into the breach.

"Very funny. But, yes, it did get pretty melodramatic for a while, at least at first. In 1998, before we left Colorado Springs, I had a malignant melanoma removed from my right arm. They used a technique called something like 'sentinel node' in which they injected some nuclear fluid in my arm and looked at lymph nodes to see if the cancer had spread. Even though it was just a needle, that was the single most painful thing I have ever experienced

Part III: Counterpoint

in my life, and so you can imagine how thrilled I was to repeat the procedure again right before the surgery. Anyway, they determined that the cancer hadn't spread, and all I would need to do was spend three months on low dose interferon, which is a kind of immunotherapy, not chemotherapy. So, phwew, bullet dodged, I thought, and life was hunky dory again.

"However, after we moved to Forest Grove, Vivian felt a lump in my arm in the exact place the melanoma had been. My new doctor sent me to a cancer specialist, whose laconic comment was, 'I guess low dose interferon doesn't work.' I now had a stage three cancerous lump in my arm, with a good likelihood it might have metastasized."

I shook my head. "Fear. Fear is all you can feel. Is that too melodramatic for you?" Alan turned his head away and pursed his lips. "I remember one oncologist telling me I had a thirty percent chance of surviving for five years. I was forty-five years old at the time, and she was telling me I had a thirty percent chance of reaching fifty. Mom had died at fifty-nine. You don't really feel pessimistic or optimistic; those emotions would be way too much effort. So, yeah, fear ruled the day, melodramatic or not. And unlike the rattlesnake incident, this fear lingered.

"I had the surgery in March of 2000. It was extensive—I still have a huge scar on my upper right arm, and I lost most of the feeling in my lower arm—but the surgeon felt it had been successful. He had 'good margins' he said. Nevertheless, given the failure of low-dose interferon, I was put on a year's treatment of high-dose interferon.

"It's not as bad as chemo, but Jesus . . . your brain turns to mush. Everything tastes like dirt: I lost thirty pounds that year. You can barely think much less talk, and you have no energy for anything. Vivian spent that year absolutely terrified that I was going to die, and putting every ounce of energy into keeping me going. Because, you see, I had to keep my job. We needed the benefits, we needed the income. Vivian even worked at the dotcom for a while, doing her job as a project manager while propping me up as technical consultant. If I could remember much of it, I suppose it would easily qualify as the worst year of my life. But now comes the kicker.

"On a Friday in May of 2001 I took my last interferon treatment. When I came to work on the following Monday, I discovered that I had been laid off. Downsizing, the company was going under, here's a very lousy severance package, good-bye. And do you know how I felt? I felt wonderful! And do you know why? Because I wasn't dead! Oh yeah, we struggled and sweated through that summer of 2001, getting COBRA benefits and unemployment. We also made some really stupid decisions, like trying to operate a little retail store, but for the most part, I didn't care. I wasn't dead! More importantly, I was alive! My brain came back, food tasted good again, and I got those thirty pounds back in a hurry. The air was sweet and the world felt good! This was a moment of clarity, like we talked about with that snake on Little Yosemite. I hated having cancer, but I think I was ultimately strengthened, not weakened, by the experience.

"I finally got another job in September, working for a startup called Medicalogic that was later bought out by GE. We had weathered the storm, money was coming in again, we'd kept our house, and it seemed like things were back on track.

"But, actually, having and surviving cancer had knocked everything off track. That intense feeling of being alive had also ignited in me the desire for more out of life. Programming was losing its attraction anyway, and I wanted meaning."

"I thought you liked programming?"

"Have you ever heard the song *Code Monkey*[1] by Jonathan Coulton?" Alan shook his head. "Well, get it off iTunes or something. In a kind of stilted simian language the song hilariously makes the point that if you think your programming job is fulfilling creatively, that's . . . well, just hooey. Maybe programming was fulfilling when I started way back in the 'cowboy' era, but by the 2000s I was clearly just a code monkey. I finally realized that I had ridden the same horse my Dad had ridden about as far as I could. I didn't want to die with my tombstone saying, 'He could really code in C++.' I wanted meaning. I wanted to do something with the new life I'd been given; with my reprieve. I wanted connectedness to that Divine Presence that had been put aside so many years before."

"So, is that when you decided to join the church, and to seek ordination?"

"Well, no, not so fast. I still had a negative and suspicious view of the church. No, in 2001 the desire was kindled, but I took some valueless detours over the next few years on my labyrinthine path, mostly because I didn't understand my desire, I had not connected it to my past, and only had an inkling of what I needed to do in the present. I was a man standing on the shore with a firm goal to get to the other side, but without a boat."

---

1. In 2006 Jonathan Coulton set out on a project to record one song a week for a whole year and posted them to his web site. He called it "A Thing a Week." *Code Monkey* arrived in week 29, and is now available on iTunes and other outlets.

Part III: Counterpoint

"I don't get it. Hadn't you been going to church all those years? I thought you were going to cleverly substitute the church for Zen and sail smoothly into the sunset."

"Hardly. And in case you're wondering, I still haven't done that. No, cancer and that heady feeling of renewed life gave me the desire, but if you want to understand how the church fits into all of this, we're going to have to go all the way back to California, before my Dad died."

"Oh, for goodness sake. For a fallow time a lot seems to have happened!"

"I warned you."

"Great. Let's find a place to stop and eat something. A place with a bathroom, please. The 'Free Continental Breakfast!' is in some distressing ways not free."

I glanced at Alan and he did look a little ill. The Wyoming sunshine had not reddened his pallor at all. It took a while to locate any kind of stopping place, and Alan began to look truly uncomfortable when we finally found a Wendy's outside of Rock Springs. I hurried him to the men's room—for once, he wasn't self-conscious about being guided—and I used the facilities as well. I met Alan outside the men's room door, and he said, "Not a Denny's, right?"

"Not a Denny's." We ordered from the counter, and sat down with our burgers and fries.

Chapter 13: Death By a Million Flea Bites

"During this fallow time," I began, between mouthfuls of hamburger, "my exposure to Christian churches was like Dr. Jekyll and Mr. Hyde over and over again. There were moments of deep and lasting inspiration, where Christ could really break through all of our human silliness and speak his simple and lasting truths; and there were times when Christ appeared to be nowhere to be found, and human silliness turned into human meanness and thoughtlessness that damaged lives and turned people away from the very Christ the church was supposed to represent.

"Most of my first encounters with Christian churches came about by dint of being a choir director, and were mostly positive, though that may have had a lot to do with the fact that I wasn't very involved except as a musician. It wasn't really the church's fault that my first marriage was so dysfunctional, and Kyle Morton had been a model of a calm, moderate, faithful pastor. Most of the churches in the 70s and 80s were perceived by me to be like that old Methodist church in Los Altos: stoic, elderly, harmless; a place to enact foreign rituals and blow the dust off the Bible from time to time. Nothing dramatically bad, and nothing dramatically interesting either. I loved the music, and I loved helping my choirs grow in repertoire and talent, but there was little or no correlation between that and growing in faith.

"In 1986, right after we got married, Vivian and I began attending Valley Presbyterian Church in Portola Valley; our second son Jeffrey was baptized there. Vivian wanted a church home for our blossoming little family, and both she and I were paid soloists in the choir of this very affluent church. The church itself was an architectural beauty, being constructed of mortared stones and large wooden beams, and it was set in the midst of

Part III: Counterpoint

a small redwood grove. The back of the chancel area, instead of being the usual cross and altar, was a gigantic clear glass window that looked out into the redwood grove. I sometimes felt sorry for the ministers, because I was certain that many in the congregation were doing exactly what I was doing during the service: soaking in the glorious redwood forest instead of listening to the magnificently dull exegesis being offered at the pulpit.

"The church employed two ministers, and in 1987 these two guys began going after each other in a very nasty and public way. I honestly do not remember what it was they were fighting about, since I still considered Sunday morning to be no more than a miniature music festival and wasn't really paying attention to other aspects of the church. But this battle was epic and after a while even I couldn't ignore it. The church began fracturing, people began taking sides, and Christ was pushed out onto the front lawn while people bickered and fought inside. There is nothing unreflective people like more than lots of drama, and I responded just like most of the church, not realizing that the reactivity of myself and the congregation just stoked the flames until all possibility of peaceful resolution was burned away. This conflict turned out to be an archetypical example of corrosive church drama that I would see played out again and again in other churches and denominations, but at the time this just reinforced for me my primal distrust of organized religion—any organized religion. It reflected what I had seen in the San Francisco Zen Center, and I began to realize just how ecumenical church conflict is.

"But as I said, these things have a Dr. Jekyll and Mr. Hyde aspect to them. The two Rev. Mr. Hydes were finally dismissed by the church's elders, and in their place were hired a reverend Dr. Jekyll and his wife: Mark and Cheryl Goodman-Morris. Mark actually was the only one hired at first, since he was male—you know Alan, if you could look at me, stop looking at me like that—but eventually Cheryl was hired as a co-pastor. As corrosive as the previous pastors had been, Mark and Cheryl were inspirational and healing both to the church as a whole, and to me in particular. This is what we professional religious types like to call a *nudge*. The church can make it so easy to walk away from it all, to abandon faith; God tends to make leaving a little harder.

"If the previous pastors had been like riding in a buckled up convertible while everybody inside was smoking, Mark and Cheryl were able to simply put the top down, douse the cigars, and drive freely in the California sunshine. See that? See how I worked in another little road metaphor . . ."

Chapter 13: Death By a Million Flea Bites

"Puleeeeze!"

"OK, well, the road still had a few speed bumps, and Mark and Cheryl had their own learning curve as husband and wife co-pastors, but it is so much easier to deal with these things in the normal course of a healthy church life if you're not also dealing with smoke and drama.

"Mark taught me my first lesson in healthy pastoral leadership one Sunday morning in 1988. It was in the spring, and as Mark attempted to give his sermon, there was a bird singing loudly and persistently in one of the redwood trees behind the chancel. After a few moments, Mark realized that everybody was listening to this bird, not his sermon, so he just stopped preaching and said, 'Let's just listen for a few moments.' After a few minutes went by, the bird began slowing down and Mark returned to the pulpit, saying, 'Well, that's the best sermon I've heard in a long time. Let us proceed to the closing hymn.' The lesson was clear: when God speaks, drop what you're doing and listen!

"And it was at that church where I was also introduced to the music of Taizé."

"Tay – what?"

"Taizé. The music originated in an ecumenical monastery near the village of Taizé, in France. In the 1960s they went from a traditional singing of the psalms to creating their own musical settings. These are short musical phrases that are repeated to encourage a contemplative state of mind. They also opened up the monastery to visitors to participate in Bible studies, work, and services built around this music and silent prayer. This became hugely popular, particularly with young people looking for a deeper spiritual experience than was offered in their local church. By the mid-seventies Taizé was hosting thousands of people every week, and they began publishing their music. People all over the world got a hold of this, and started doing Taizé-style services in churches and retreat centers. Mark and Cheryl offered a couple of Taizé services at Valley Presbyterian, and I was intrigued, and began learning the music myself. But when Vivian and I moved to Snohomish in July of 1989, we also left Taizé behind for a couple of years.

"We left our Presbyterian church behind with some sadness when we moved to Snohomish, but also with a positive feeling that church could be done well and faithfully given the right pastoral leadership. To someone not familiar with the church—like you, Alan—this might seem obvious, but in Protestant churches in particular this concept can be confusing. Most Protestant churches have some kind of a concept of the 'ministry of all believers,' and many have put polity constraints on ministers in order to encourage the laity to take more responsibility for the life and health of the church. However, there is a long tradition regarding ministers that predates Protestantism that grants the minister supreme authority within his—don't pretend to look at me like that again, Alan; it's been *his* exclusively until very recently—supreme authority within his church or cathedral. No matter what the church's polity says, congregations for the most part still assume this supreme authority on the part of their minister. No matter how matrixed leadership in a church may be, the old axiom that 'crap flows downhill' is as true in a church as anywhere else. And, to be fair, it is equally true that milk and honey flow downhill too. The health, maturity, integrity and faithfulness of the minister in any church will flow downhill into the rest of the church leadership and into the congregation in a way that, by some law of organizational physics, it cannot flow uphill. Healthy churches have healthy ministers; unhealthy churches either have unhealthy ministers or have some poor slob who is desperately trying to clean up the mess left by the previous guy."

"You do realize, don't you, that you're telling me you have chosen a profession in which the central rubric is 'crap flows downhill'?"

"No, Alan, that is *not* the central rubric of ministry, even if it sometimes can feel that way. Let me give you another example.

"Shortly after arriving in Snohomish, I was hired as the music director for First Presbyterian Church in Everett. This was again another architectural beauty, built of brick and stone, and it stood on top of the hill in Everett like an old-time New England church, complete with the lichen and moss that clung to the stone in the damp climate of the Northwest. On the first Sunday that Vivian and I went there to check it out, the entire chancel area was under construction and covered with a thick layer of visqueen. My first thought was 'uh-oh,' but on that August day two of the choir members did a duet for special music, standing on the far right of the church because there was no chancel to use as a stage, and they were marvelous! Vivian and I agreed that any church that could field such talent on a very 'off' Sunday was worth being a part of. It was on this same Sunday that the deal was sealed when we met the pastor for the first time.

"Someone once remarked that if central casting ever needed a minister, they should call the Rev. Dr. Edwin C. Coon. With his silver hair, tall, rugged good looks and rich baritone voice, he completely looked and sounded the part. His sermons indicated that he also had the spiritual

Chapter 13: Death By a Million Flea Bites

depth of a deeply faithful man, and nothing that happened over the two years we attended First Presbyterian ever indicated anything different. He and his wife Betty also had a great sense of humor and had a way of making everyone they came in contact with feel welcome.

"Ed Coon lives within my pantheon of 'the most important people in my life,' and he brought faithful Christianity alive for me in a powerful way. I'm sure Ed has done much more important things in his life, but not for me. He finally convinced me to take a class in Christian faith that ultimately led me, at the age of thirty-six, to being baptized. Ed was genuine, optimistic, inspirational, and a great preacher, the kind of minister I can only dream of emulating."

I paused for a moment, leaving a gap that Alan immediately filled with, "Why do I sense there's a 'but' coming?"

I sighed. "Sadly, there is. First Presbyterian was an old, downtown church, weighed down by years of tradition. It was the church where the elite of Everett attended. Had my mom been alive, she would have been thrilled to know that this was the church that Scoop Jackson had attended."

Alan shook his head, not recognizing the name, "Scoop Jackson?"

"Yeah, the senator and presidential candidate from Washington State. I guess not a lot of people remember him anymore. I think my mom and six other people supported him when he ran for president in 1972. The point is, this was the church that was attended by senators and the other members of the upper crust in Everett. And although the church had a duly constituted governing board, called the 'session' as prescribed by the Presbyterian Book of Order, the church was actually run by a group of trustees who were accountable to no one except tradition. Ed wanted to change this so that the church would be run the way it should be under Presbyterian polity, so naturally the trustees decided it was time to get rid of Ed. They began a vicious 'dump the pastor' campaign, called in outside consultants to tell the church how dysfunctional it was under Ed's leadership, trashed him publically, organized secret meetings, and eventually forced him to retire."

"Ouch! It sounds like Mr. Hyde showed up!"

"With a vengeance. I was heartbroken, and I resigned as music director and left the church, convinced that the church was an instrument of evil, even if contained a few genuine followers of Christ like Ed."

"Well, it sounds like in this situation crap flowed uphill."

"I guess crap can flow any direction it wants to, but in this case the problem was that the minister wasn't *at* the top of the hill: the real authority

Part III: Counterpoint

was held outside the church's own polity by that group of trustees. Another hallmark of an unhealthy church is a church with secret authority, confused authority. For a minister it's like having a revolver pointed at your head all the time, and you don't know if there's a bullet in the chamber or not."

Again, Alan shook his head. "None of this is really convincing me that you've picked an appropriate profession!"

"Well, at the same time all of this crap was flowing, God was saving me through music."

"Do you realize how ridiculous that sounds?"

"No, no. It might sound silly, but it's pretty much true. It is true. Just before retiring, Ed and I took a trip together down to Portland to attend a seminar for Presbyterian pastors and musicians. Ed and I had a great talk as we motored down Interstate-5 about the difficulties he was facing, and how shaken and puzzled he was by the whole thing. We stayed at one of his kids' houses in Camus, and the next day headed over the river into downtown Portland for the seminar. The seminar was pretty good and, like most seminars of this nature, consisted of sessions describing resources and techniques available to pastors and church musicians to enhance worship. But in the evening, the host church put on a worship service for the participants, and little did I know this simple service would be life changing.

"First Presbyterian Church in downtown Portland is yet another architectural beauty, particularly on the inside. The beams in the sanctuary are built in beautifully polished dark wood, and there is not a straight line to be found. The wood has been carefully shaped to curve and swoop around the balcony, and wooden arches support the ceiling. The sanctuary floor is made of lighter wooden planks, highlighted by pews that look like dark chocolate set amidst caramel. It is truly stunning, and I suppose all that wood and outstanding craftsmanship was particularly appealing to my Zen-Druid side. But in spite of its great beauty, God did not grab me with architecture on that evening.

"Pastors cherish opportunities to worship as worshippers, not as leaders, so this service was well attended and appreciated. Eventually, we came to the part of the service where communion was being served, and as the participants lined up to receive the elements, the organist began playing *Jesus, Remember Me*. This was a popular song from Taizé that I had learned back in Portola Valley, but at that service in Portland I finally 'got it.' The music became a prayer, repeated over and over again; 'Jesus, remember me, when you come into your kingdom.' It's a little hard to describe, but

Chapter 13: Death By a Million Flea Bites

suddenly these pastors and musicians, who often spend most of a worship service worrying if the candles are lit or the choir is in place or if they're prepared for their sermon, found themselves able to open their hearts and let the spirit of God rush in, rush through them to be carried out on their voices and breathed in by the person next to them.

"I was in tears. In that moment I was only in the moment, but I later realized that I had uncovered that missing link between music and spirit. Music could be more than satisfying, more than entertaining, more than attractional. I now realize that I had truly experienced that which had eluded me in music school: the mystery of music melded with the mystery of the Divine Presence, like tea leaves into hot water. It would be the keystone in the archway leading me to ministry; the first piece of the puzzle that connected a contemplative practice that actually spoke to me with the life of the Spirit. Although not yet completely solved, it was the beginning of answers to the conundrum described by mom just before she died: can you be contemplative and active at the same time?"

"Sorry," Alan said, "but I think that your mom's conundrum also begs the question of whether you can be both or either within conventional religion. She ultimately was disillusioned by both Buddhism and Christianity and described them as nearly polar opposites. And you've just described this Tay . . . tez . . . whatever, community in France that operates on the outside of established Christian religious structures. I guess I'm still not seeing where conventional church fits in."

"Well, at that time, I didn't either. To be honest, I kept attending church because Vivian insisted that we bring up our kids with a religious background, and I grudgingly agreed with her. But for many years I continued to limit my participation to music only. I had found something with Taizé, but lost something else when Ed was railroaded out of his church. But over the course of the next fifteen years, we found only a few churches that didn't sooner or later devolve into some kind of toxic, divisive situation. Honestly, we began to wonder if it wasn't us, if we were bringing some kind of poisonous karma into these churches. But we began to observe that corrosive interactions in church were all too common, even in churches we didn't attend.

"After leaving First Presbyterian, we sought refuge in the Snohomish Methodist Church. It was an ancient white clapboard church that had been placed on the Historic Register. We enjoyed it for a while, but on Mother's Day one year the pastor gave a gruesome sermon on what should have been

Part III: Counterpoint

a happy celebration of Motherhood, something quite close to Vivian's heart at the time with our two young kids. Somehow the sermon involved a grandchild killing their grandfather, which was just way too much for Vivian. She politely stayed through the end of the service, but as we exited the church she said 'I'm never coming back here.' I meekly followed her, mumbling, 'Uh, yeah. Me too.' We picked up the kids at Sunday School and in fact never went back. Being married to a redhead is nothing if not entertaining."

"Again, you're not really convincing me. You put church off at arm's length for good reason. So, did you wake up one morning with a headache and decide you really wanted more?"

"Well, you're right about the headache. Even when we moved to Colorado Springs in 1995, the church continued to be a Dr. Jekyll and Mr. Hyde experience."

"At last! Colorado Springs! Hold that thought, and let's get out of here!"

We tossed our trash into a barrel, drove across the street to get gas and a bag of very cheap, sugary cookies, and quickly returned to the freeway. It was now past noon and the rocks and sand shimmered as the heat came up.

"Colorado Springs indeed. We didn't leave Snohomish because of the church, you know, we left because of the rain. Still, I think our time in The Springs was the apogee of my journey through suburban living. I'm not trying to be snide; Vivian and I actually were very happy for most of our time in The Springs. But we did not escape Dr. Jekyll and Mr. Hyde in our church experience, and continued to be frustrated by a pattern of competent, inspirational pastors followed by incompetent jerks."

"Yikes! Still, I've heard Colorado Springs was a very religious town. Wasn't Focus on the Family down there? Yet your experience wasn't a hundred percent hunky-dory, was it? Is it just because you were sticking with the Methodist Church?"

"No, no. Other churches, even the big charismatic non-denominational ones that the Springs was famous for, had their share of issues and corrosion. The Methodist church we first attended was a relatively new church, planted on the west side of town as the suburbs grew up over there. The pastor, Deb Olenyik—another entry in my pantheon of heroes—was a very professional, very inspirational pastor. Vivian worked as the church secretary and witnessed her share of craziness as people interacted with the pastor. These are the kind of interactions that, if handled poorly, can start the corrosive process, but Deb handled them all lovingly, firmly, and with a true pastoral attitude that kept the church healthy. I, of course, was skirting

Chapter 13: Death By a Million Flea Bites

the edges with the music department, and eventually went to another Methodist church on the other side of town to serve as music director. I served there for just a year, and by the time I came back, Deb had moved on and had been replaced by—you guessed it—another Reverend Mr. Hyde."

"So, here we go again."

"Yeah. Things got so bad with this new guy that the leaders of the church actually withheld payments to the Conference until the Conference paid attention to them. Methodist churches pay a portion of their income to the Conference, called *apportionments*, and this church leadership put all of their apportionments into an escrow account instead of paying it to the Conference, which really got their attention. The Conference finally 'reassigned' the Reverend Mr. Hyde. The church eventually healed up and is now a very healthy church, but by then, Vivian and I were long gone.

"I know I should be more forgiving, particularly since we were going to United Methodist churches, but even at the distance I kept I could see how this bipolar church experience was really hurting people, damaging their faith, creating anger and driving people not only away from church, but away from seeking spiritual meaning. The good pastor sets them up for a meaningful, inspirational faith journey, then the bad pastor comes along and sinks the ship."

"Again: awfully dramatic!"

"You're right. Too dramatic, really. Only a few churches actually end up sinking right away. But it's like death by a million flea bites. When a church goes through some toxic, corrosive episode, it generally recovers to some extent: changes are made, forgiveness happens and so forth. But three things happen with each flea bite. First, some people leave that church and find a different church home that, at least for the time being, doesn't have the drama. This is a kind of redistribution of the faithful that happens all the time. Second, someone will inevitably walk away and not come back. They're burned out on church, it doesn't lift them up, they don't want the fights, whatever. So no matter how often the faithful get redistributed, there is almost always a net loss. And last, and probably worst, the recovered toxic church now has a bad reputation and new seekers might find themselves reluctant to explore their faith at that venue. So as time goes on, new people don't attend and the faithful get older and older, so that even if the toxic reputation has faded, it is replaced with a new reputation as being an 'old people's church.' I'm not making this up, Alan, I've seen this pattern too many times, and it has been written about innumerable times. Can the church survive a single flea bite?

Part III: Counterpoint

Of course. Can the Church survive the millions of flea bites that have come over the last fifty years? I'm just not sure . . ."

Alan looked puzzled. "Jeez, bud, are you trying to talk yourself out of this? Let's face it, for the last two hundred miles you've done nothing but lay out a case against joining up with the church."

"Maybe I am. It's a pretty central issue, don't you think? Every time this pattern occurs in a church, some people do lose faith and walk away, feeling damaged by the one institution that should be trying to keep them safe, spiritually. The Good Shepherd, right? This has been the pattern of long term corrosion in the institutional church for fifty years, maybe more. Obviously, not every church has died out, but almost every church has felt the effects of this corrosion, and that really doesn't help in a society that is increasingly skeptical about the church anyway. I might be able to help with one flea bite, but a million . . .?"

"Well, yeah," Alan said. "I mean, what I don't get, is what's in it for you? Why would you stay? Why subject yourself to all that crap, no matter where it flows from? Isn't that the way it works with church? There's this big buffet out there with every conceivable flavor of church on it; if you don't like one you move on to the next. Redistribute yourself. Reinvent yourself."

"The buffet is great metaphor for a Chinese restaurant, but I'm not really sure it works for church. Nevertheless, it's the metaphor that Vivian and I followed for years—most of our adult lives, really—but I was beginning to understand that it might be problematic. Redistributing the faithful also redistributes the problem. For one thing, I've used this Dr. Jekyll and Mr. Hyde metaphor primarily in regard to pastoral leadership, but that does not excuse congregations and individuals in the laity from their responsibilities either. There are individuals in congregations who can be real muckrakers too, and I think that churches, in an effort to be 'nice,' too often are not effective in dealing with muckraking, which leads to corrosion in the church body. And one way the church doesn't deal with its problems is that people just give up and move on down the buffet, often carrying the corrosion with them.

"Good, healthy churches are just like good, healthy marriages. They're good and healthy because the participants work at it all the time, even during the hard times. But nowadays people will walk away from marriages too easily just because they can, because other relationships are so easily available: a kind of relationship buffet. And I think I walked away from too many churches because of the existence of the same kind of religious buffet. But just like many people learn out of the pain of divorce that the grass

Chapter 13: Death By a Million Flea Bites

really isn't greener on the other side, so it is with church. A weak commitment produces more churn, more upheaval, and a weakening of the central component of the church. Many writers have written about how church is irrelevant in the twenty-first century; how it's boring and the music is old fashioned and it doesn't do this or do that very well. These complaints are analogous to the excuses used in describing a crumbling marriage. But these complaints are most often about the exteriors of the church, the embellishments, the accoutrements, and as such don't really address the core problem of a lack of commitment to the Christian path. Exteriors, embellishments and accoutrements can always be changed, just like people in a marriage can alter the things about their lives that aren't working. But you have to be committed to the marriage itself to make it work. If all I ever did was walk away from churches with problems then all I ever did was contribute to those problems."

"No matter what?"

"What do you mean?"

"Well, you walked away from your first marriage, and I can't say I blame you. That grass was dead. So, are you saying you should stick it out with a church no matter what the condition of the grass?"

Alan could really be annoying, particularly when he was right. I sighed. "Well, it's not really black and white, is it? Certainly, one is justified in ending an abusive relationship, or a truly loveless relationship. But breaking commitment should never be easy, and I think it has become far too easy in the modern church. Jesus tried to teach peacemaking and reconciliation, very much so at the interpersonal level, and Paul emphasizes over and over again the need for the people within the Body of Christ—the church—to embrace differences and diversity as the various components of a well-functioning body. But, again like a marriage, I think people want to avoid the pain and conflict that inevitably comes with diversity and change, when it is oh so much easier to simply swap out churches like we swap out partners. Or why not avoid it altogether by simply leaving the church entirely?"

"Well, why not? Should we be seeking out pain and conflict?"

"Yes! All growth and change involves pain, but no growth and change leads only to stagnation and death. Churches die because they stagnate, weakened to change because of too many flea bites; relationships also die because they stagnate. The only possible way to move forward, to live out the transformation of the spirit that is central to the Christian message, is to undergo painful change. And while such change is theoretically possible alone, people tend to seek out other people for support and guidance, particularly in tumultuous times, thus producing faith communities: churches. Almost all of the conflict in churches revolves around change: either actual change itself or resistance to the necessity for change, including change required on the part of the pastor. In other words, the avoidance of pain causes pain. Well, if I had avoided the pain of my cancer treatments, I'd be dead. But nevertheless I and many others have spent a lot of time trying to avoid the pain of churches in transition, trying to avoid the flea bites. And just as people are trying to avoid the pain of repairing and growing their marriages, and the divorce rate is skyrocketing, I don't think it is a coincidence that this is happening at the same time the church is withering. The avoidance of pain is synonymous to a lack of commitment, which ultimately causes more damage than committing to work through the pain in the first place."

Again, silence ensued as Alan tried to chew through this latest outburst on my part. I was beginning to feel sorry for him. In some ways the avoidance of commitment has become so engrained in our society that I might as well have been talking to Alan in Martian. Nevertheless, I continued, "Changing your mind at a Chinese restaurant because there are too many choices is far different from wandering aimlessly forever on an unlit faith path. When you find the light, stick to it, just like when you find your soul mate, stick to her! This is actually a very Biblical concept. Not only is the association between human love and the love of God outlined beautifully in such books as *The Song of Solomon*, but a major theme in both testaments of the Bible is the consequences of faithlessness and the rewards of faithfulness. Bad things happen to people who fail to keep their commitments. Those who maintain their commitments to God are rewarded, often in very human ways."

Alan finally emerged from his musings. "Now I feel kind of shallow. I never really thought before about how, just because it's easy to walk away does not necessarily make it right. But you kept doing it anyway. You walked away from your first marriage, you walked away from all of those churches. You walked away from Zen when it got hard, you walked away from Pinecrest; you even more or less walked away from music. This whole house of cards about connecting with the past and finding your roots is going straight down the toilet, brother. What do you say to that?"

I knew this challenge was coming, and I had an answer prepared. I wasn't about to let on to Alan that all of this might just be wishful thinking,

Chapter 13: Death By a Million Flea Bites

but I had to try it out. "Well, here's another road metaphor for you. One of Steven Spielberg's first movies, *Duel,* was about a guy, played by Dennis Weaver, on a car trip who cuts off a giant tanker truck on the highway, and the truck begins to pursue him relentlessly. Weaver keeps running away, trying various tricks to avoid the truck, to get away from it and its mysterious driver whom we never see. But the truck just keeps on pursuing him. Weaver gets more and more desperate and is more and more filled with fear, but he can't get away. Finally, at the end of the movie, he stops running away. He turns around, faces his fear and challenges the evil truck, defeating it in a dramatic crash that costs him nearly everything. That's what I did. Not so dramatically, I suppose, but I stopped running away."

Alan snorted. "I'm not even going to try and figure out the symbolism of a giant tanker truck pursuing someone into a spiritual life. Or a swarm of fleas, for that matter. But what changed? Did you just screw your courage to the sticking point, hitch up your pants and head west, or did something happen that turned you around to face the giant tanker truck of your fears?"

"Something happened. Something happened to Vivian, actually, that finally got me turned around. It involves one more Dr. Jekyll and Mr. Hyde story, I'm afraid, but it will be the last."

Alan sighed. "One more? OK, lay on, Macduff."

Once again on this journey I was struck by how the landscape seemed to reflect the contours of my story. I-80 crosses the Continental Divide twice as it skirts the ridges at the southern end of the Great Divide Basin. We had already passed over the western divide, sped as quickly as we could through Rawlins, home of the now infamous 'sleep-optional' motel, and were making good time towards Laramie. The Great Divide, I thought, that separates East from West. How many thousands of pilgrims had crossed this same divide over the years, some crawling, some speeding towards new lives? How appropriate, I thought, as we drove into the stories that represented the Great Divide in my life. *Too dramatic, too dramatic*, I thought. Divide or not, the road leads home, and driving west to east towards Colorado was going home for me. It was the direction I'd always wanted to be on, but had only recently come to realize I had been going that direction all along.

Chapter 14: Nexus II

"When we moved to Forest Grove in September of 1999, we bought a house which turned out to be right across the street from the home of the choir director for the Forest Grove United Church of Christ. She saw our music books coming off of the moving van and immediately came over and asked us to join the choir. So, we ended up attending the Forest Grove UCC for the next several years.

"At about the same time, in 2001, Vivian finished up her training at the prestigious Shalem Institute in Maryland and began to pursue a private practice as a Spiritual Director." I stopped and laughed a little self-consciously. "I don't know if prestigious is the right word, since one of the founding principles of the Institute is humility before God; but nevertheless, Shalem is one of the few places in America with a real seriousness towards ecumenical contemplative practice. It was founded and run by some real luminaries amongst American contemplatives: Tilden Edwards, Rosemary Dougherty and the late Gerry May. Studying there really brought Vivian's contemplative practice and path into focus. Again, I had trouble following her on the contemplative path in any way except through Taizé services, but I had deep respect for that path and still considered it a vital component to spiritual growth. In the early 2000s this remained an area of confusion for me: if this was such a vital component, why was I so uninterested in meditation? The answer, I think, came later, but as we settled into life in Forest Grove, that part remained Vivian's story.

"The Forest Grove UCC was another church in transition. The previous pastor of 25 years retired on the Sunday immediately prior to the Sunday we started attending, and for the first year we were there we had some

Chapter 14: Nexus II

interim pastors. We liked the choir and our new neighbors, and the church was open and welcoming, with an active youth group for our growing kids. With a few other folks we started a rock 'n' roll band and introduced the bemused congregation to some contemporary Christian music.

"Vivian began exploring with the denomination the possibility of becoming a commissioned minister in the UCC, with an emphasis on spiritual formation through contemplative practice. Vivian had been leading workshops, had given seminars at various Conference gatherings, and had formed a Conference wide spirituality leadership group. Commissioning seemed the next logical step. Commissioning required a degree or certificate in the field for which you were being commissioned, which Vivian had from Shalem, as well as experience in that field, but there were no specific requirements for commissioning in spirituality: Vivian would be the first.

"The UCC denomination was an attempt to unite Congregational churches around a common polity, which always seemed to me a rather futile effort considering how Congregational churches were historically famous for being proudly independent. This mismatched marriage of independent churches caused the UCC polity to be confusing and rather toothless, which produced the predictable result: in order to make up for a lack of a clear direction in polity, leaders within the UCC had to take up the slack by assuming authority not specifically granted to them by their denomination. The leaders of the conferences within the UCC were called Conference Ministers, and the quality or arbitrariness of their leadership was based almost entirely on this assumed authority. From out of this mess, the Conference Ministers were able to try and grind up Vivian's efforts."

"Why do I get the feeling that crap was about to start flowing downhill?"

"Well, you would be right. In this case, though, it wasn't from the local church or the pastor, who actually really supported Vivian in her efforts, but from the two Conference Ministers. Vivian had faithfully jumped through all the institutional hoops in order to be commissioned, and had at last been able to schedule an 'Ecclesiastical Council' as the final hoop. This was a gathering, usually within the candidate's home church, where friends, congregation members, clergy and really just about anybody could come and question the candidate to determine their eligibility. At the conclusion, the candidate leaves the room and the assembly votes as to whether they should be approved. It's a big deal, and since the questions aren't monitored, anyone can ask you pretty much anything. Consequently, candidates spend a great deal of time studying, praying and reflecting in order to be prepared

Part III: Counterpoint

for this ordeal. There was probably no one on the planet better prepared for this sort of thing than Vivian, so you can just imagine her shock when, on the day before her scheduled Ecclesiastical Council, the Conference Ministers called and cancelled it, no reason given.

"Oh my God! You've got to be kidding! Why?"

"It was a little mysterious, but basically the two Conference Ministers, exercising their arbitrary authority, decided they didn't like Vivian. I suspected they thought she wasn't liberal enough for that very liberal denomination, and they seemed to consider spirituality a little bit subversive and confusing. In fact, no reason was ever given, and the decision was arbitrary and extremely hurtful. People who had not been notified of the cancellation actually showed up for the thing, causing painful humiliation for Vivian as she met them at the doors of the church and shooed them away. She then had to go and meet with the Conference Ministers and defend herself within a conflict that they had created. Our pastor, God bless him, went with Vivian to these meetings and he too was shocked by this arbitrary use of authority. Lots of smoke and drama. Mr. Hyde in the form of denominational leaders."

Alan sighed, exasperated. "This sounds in some ways like the situation with Richard Baker at Zen Center. No molestation, I hope, but another example of leaders in religious positions abusing their authority."

"Yeah. Hell of a way to connect with my past, huh? And like I said back then, it's one thing when this happens to you; you can deal with it, process it. But when it happens to your wife, your soul mate . . . well, I was furious. Absolutely furious, with no way to act on it. This was Vivian's professional career and her life's work ground under foot just at the big moment. As much as I wanted to, I couldn't just go and punch those Conference Ministers in the nose. Just another example of the church gone wrong, and I finally hit the wall in regards to church. All of that walking away over the years, and I finally decided I had to fish or cut bait. I had to either walk away from the church for good, or get in there and do something about it."

Alan snorted, which caused him to cough for a few moments. He really didn't sound too good, and I began to wonder if this might be more than a lack of sleep. Finally, he croaked out, "I would have walked away. Who needs that kind of grief? You and Vivian could have simply pursued spirituality stuff on your own, made your own peace with God, done your own spiritual wandering, without having to get side-tracked and punished by the big institution."

Chapter 14: Nexus II

"Yes. We could just have taken care of ourselves, worked to make ourselves better. Brought peace to our own lives. Have I mentioned self, myself enough? Yes, I could have become like a private spiritual art collector, gathering up all the spiritual things with value and hanging them on my own wall so only I could see them, only I could benefit from them. Let everybody else get whatever they can, sink or swim, 'cause I got mine!"

"OK, OK, I get it! But why not start your own church, share your faith that way?"

"We thought about that some. Maybe that would have been best, I don't know. But why reinvent the wheel? Our brand and style of Christianity, the things that brought me and Vivian spiritual growth and fulfillment, weren't particularly radical. I don't think we had any astonishing new ideas upon which to build a following. I also think the computer engineer in me was very annoyed to see a system running so poorly. The message of Christ is powerful, meaningful and life changing, yet traditional church systems were eroding that power and meaning primarily through mediocre—or worse—execution of their primary task. Christ wants us to be better, not worse, and most definitely not mediocre. If the computer companies I had worked for were that bad at producing and sustaining their products they would have died out long ago. The church has the best product ever, one that practically sells itself, yet the church is withering. When Vivian got kicked in the stomach by the UCC, I guess I just picked up that old cliché of deciding whether I wanted to be a part of problem or a part of the solution."

"Whoa, whoa, wait a minute. Isn't that a little grandiose? You're just going to jump in and save the church?"

I blushed a little, not that Alan could tell. "I guess that does sound a little arrogant. I'm not some latter-day day Martin Luther who wants to single-handedly reform and revive the church. Though I daresay there aren't many ministers out there who haven't at one point or another thought about what they would do if they could be in charge of the church. I do remember thinking at the time that I could do church a lot better than 'those guys,' but a somewhat more considered version is that I would like to emulate those good, inspirational Dr. Jekyll pastors I've encountered in the past.

"The church holds a sacred trust. It retains all of the things that make up the artifacts of sanctity: the scriptures, the wisdom, the spiritual paths and so forth. But it must also breathe life into these artifacts in the light of each new generation so that the Divine Presence remains a living presence, not a musky museum piece. I finally realized how important this was, and

Part III: Counterpoint

that it was important for me to be a part of the life-giving aspects of the church, regardless of my concerns about the corrosive part. No, I don't really have grandiose plans to 'save' the church all by myself, but if I can be at a minimum one less flea, that's helpful, right?"

Alan grunted and said, "Great. We've gone from the central rubric of the church being 'crap flows downhill' to 'I wanna be one less flea.'"

I had to laugh at that: it did sound a little silly. "OK, well, it sounds a little better than being one more Mr. Hyde. And don't you think that one more Dr. Jekyll, one less Mr. Hyde, could only improve the system? And not just one less flea, but one more positive voice. The anger I felt over the poor leadership and nearly anti-Christian behavior of some in the church gave way over time to the realization that I could only really affect my little corner of the world. And I realized that there really were many out there in and around the church who cared about the sacred trust and who watched with equal dismay at the corrosive work of the few Mr. Hydes. The pursuit of meaning, of actively seeking, meant walking towards it, not just not walking away. And it's not just a question of stopping the church from running over people like Vivian, it's trying to be in a position to foster people like Vivian, who are seeking in their own way the same meaning through faith.

"But I didn't just run out the next day, quit my job and sign up with the church. It took me years to completely turn the corner. And we did walk away, sort of, one more time. We stayed at that UCC church and tried to work through the problems with the denomination, and Vivian did finally have her Ecclesiastical Council, where she was approved unanimously. But the UCC wasn't done with her. They had gotten rid of the two Mr. Hyde Conference Ministers and replaced them with a single Conference Minister, who promptly told Vivian he wasn't sure if she had really been commissioned, and withheld her certificate. It became sadly clear that although we had tried not to walk away from the UCC, the UCC had walked away from us with determination. If I was going to enter the church to try and be a positive voice, it wasn't going to be with the United Church of Christ. So, when a position for a Choir Director opened up at the Methodist church in the neighboring town of Hillsboro, I took that job, and we moved our spiritual home to the United Methodist Church."

"It's funny, don't you think," Alan said, "that you ended up in a denomination that had a church right next door to you when you were a kid? A church you never attended, but just used as a blind for sneaking a smoke?"

Chapter 14: Nexus II

I had to laugh at that too. "Yeah, that's occurred to me. Is there a deeper meaning hidden there somewhere? Did I unconsciously associate Methodism with something memorable, albeit very covert, in my childhood? Actually, I don't really think so. There are United Methodist churches everywhere. Fewer now, of course, but it would have been hard to grow up anywhere in the sixties and not be within a few miles of a Methodist church. But I also think there was a certain inevitability about it, because when I started at Hillsboro United Methodist, my efforts at ministry were immediately supported by the congregation and the pastor. It was like seeing an opening in the traffic while driving on the highway and just taking it.

"I was encouraged enough that I decided I would take a class at the only mainline Protestant seminary in the Northwest called The Northwest House of Theological Studies. Classes met on the campus of Willamette University in Salem, about an hour's drive south of Forest Grove. Classes were designed precisely for people like me who had day jobs and were approaching the task of getting a Master of Divinity degree as a second career. I was so nervous about doing this that I didn't tell Vivian about it until after I had actually registered for a class, which really caught her off guard. I think I probably had given her the impression that I was going to choose the opposite direction—away from religion—while she continued to work and teach professionally in the area of Spiritual Direction. Nevertheless, I enrolled in a six week intensive course in theology taught by Dr. Dell Brown, and drove down to Salem every Friday night after work to attend the Friday/Saturday course. Dell was the best possible first teacher of theology for me, being a solid United Methodist, but also somewhat out of the mainstream as a process theologian. He had an open mind and a good sense of humor. My favorite memory is after he read one of my bizarre papers, one of my first attempts to pull together my unusual upbringing in a Christian theological format, he remarked, 'Well! It's no surprise to me that your mother was a Buddhist!'

"That class was enough to encourage me to continue my studies. I found Dell's comment about my mother being Buddhist rather encouraging as well, and the pieces of my upbringing that I had for so long felt had been abandoned now started to fall into place. That need I had felt for that connection, that sense that I was living a whole life, began to occur more and more. I still needed something to convince me that not only was this the right path, but that it was a path I had been on forever. You get it, right Alan? You get that I wasn't only seeking God and faith, but that I was also

Part III: Counterpoint

seeking the meaning of my life's trajectory? You've pounded me with the accusation that I had forgotten or pushed aside all of those marvelous influences of my youth, and at that point of my life, a cancer survivor and a newly minted seeker, I was wondering the same thing."

"So, connect the dots for me. Right now I see a man who is all emotion but little connection."

"Yeah, that's actually pretty true. I think with something like this, you need to be convinced emotionally before you can later find the language to express it. OK, you're going to laugh, and this time I deserve it, but one of these moments of connectedness occurred in a Starbucks in Salem." Alan did indeed laugh, and I couldn't blame him. "Yeah, in that most prosaic of places. I had been reading J. Phillip Newell's book *Listening for the Heartbeat of God*,[1] which was my first introduction to Celtic Christianity. Actually, the discovery of Celtic Christianity was a tremendous influence on me in and of itself. The Celts have a beautiful way of connecting creation, the natural world, with Christian spirituality. I really liked, and continue to like, that aesthetic approach to our relationship with God through nature. But in one chapter he discusses the life of a fifth century Celtic monk named Pelagius. Pelagius had moved to Rome from Britain, where he taught Christian morality to young women. He also wrote many treatises, and in some he put forth a notion that humans had the ability to turn towards God of their own free will. A powerful Bishop, Augustine of Hippo, decided this was scandalous. The free will of men, Augustine declared, could only be used to do evil: all that was good in the world could only come from God, and only God could turn a man's heart by grace towards salvation. To me, Augustine's position seemed horrible: if man only had free will to do evil, man did not have free will. Augustine's arguments, expressed in a couple of his own treatises, both trashed Pelagius and laid the groundwork for the onerous concept of original sin. Pelagius had no real desire to get into a fight with the powerful Bishop of Hippo, but nevertheless had to defend himself twice in church courts in Jerusalem against charges of heresy. Both times, he was found not guilty. Augustine was so infuriated that, when a new Pope was installed, he convinced the new Pope, without evidence, to excommunicate the Celtic monk *in absentia*."

"Wait a minute, wait a minute." Alan moaned incredulously, "Are you saying that crap has been flowing downhill since the fifth century?"

---

1. Newell, *Listening for The Heartbeat*, 20.

Chapter 14: Nexus II

"Long before that, I imagine. Anyway, Pelagius couldn't have cared less and, fed up with Rome, tradition has it that he returned home to Britain to retire. Pelagius seemed like a hero to me. Someone who searched for wholeness rather than orthodoxy, someone who believed in an interactive God, not a puppet-master God. Someone who believed that God's spirit is interwoven with creation like tea leaves and hot water, and not mitigated or controlled through the church. I was quite ferocious and passionate about this at the time—still am, mostly—but then primarily because it resonated with my distrust of the church. History has treated Pelagius badly precisely because he challenged the authority of church teachings. Good for him! So, by the time I got to the last sentences of this chapter in Newell's book, my Caramel Macchiato long gone, I was quite worked up. The last sentence says something like 'and Pelagius is said to have retired to his home in Bangor, Wales.'

"I felt like I had been hit by a truck. My head exploded. Without proof, I knew that I had stood in the very same stone circle near Bangor, Wales that Pelagius had stood in 1,500 years ago. I was sobbing my eyes out, trying to hide it from the other customers, trying to ignore the odd looks from the barista. How could it be that a chance encounter with a stone circle on my one and only trip to Wales thirty years before could be a bridge to a deeply meaningful spiritual path? It made no sense! It was a mystery! Nevertheless, I felt strongly that long elusive connection with the earlier part of my life. I had visited that site in Wales for a reason. It didn't matter at all if Pelagius had actually ever stood in that very same stone circle, what mattered was that I was now connected by that experience to a conviction of faith that was shared with the old Celtic monk. An emotional connection, to be sure. I wasn't a stooge in God's creation and subject to a whimsical Overlord; free will was God's greatest gift precisely because it makes humanity like a junior partner in God's kingdom. We can participate *with* God in God's purposes."

Again, Alan had to chew this over for a minute. We had now passed over the second version of the Continental Divide and were approaching Laramie. Finally, he asked, "Weren't the Celts really into nature worship? I mean, Free Will really sounds intellectual: weren't you more attracted by the association with Pinecrest, with your Druid self and your emotional grounding in nature?"

"Of course that's true. I had been brought up in a way that emphasized being a part of nature, being in it. But I had thought that Christianity only offered a doctrine of separateness from nature. It's the whole 'dominion over' stuff out of Genesis, whereas I was brought up with a more 'participate with'

Part III: Counterpoint

attitude. Yeah, the more I think about it, the more I think you're right, for once. What a relief to find out that I could, within Christianity, continue my beliefs about connectedness with all of creation! That's a very strong tie to Pinecrest and the hours I spent with the rocks and lizards and trees. That tiny Welsh stone circle outlined the wholeness, the completeness I sought. I guess I can only articulate it now, but yeah, that must have flashed through me way back at that old Starbucks, because I'm certain that was the moment when I realized I could authentically embrace Christianity. Up until then, I felt like an outsider in many ways. Many of my admittedly not fully formed theological views seemed so out of the mainstream and contrary to church doctrine, yet here was a tradition and history that honored the path of Christ and remained true to the Gospels without separating the believer from the very creation God had placed him in. What I had felt instinctively as a child was now validated and connected up to me as an adult both emotionally and rationally, all because of a silly Welsh stone circle. I love that stone circle!" I started laughing, and burst out singing *The Circle of Life* in a loud voice. Again, Alan was annoyed.

"Please, please don't do that."

"What?" I gasped between laughs. "Who doesn't like *The Lion King?*"

"Me. I don't like *The Lion King.*"

I just kept on singing, but after a few minutes I had to stop; I was laughing too hard. But when I looked at Alan, he seemed genuinely distressed. Nothing provokes laughter like laughter, but Alan's unexpected gloom cut mine off like a knife. Finally I said, "Hey man. Sorry, sometimes I just get carried away. It was one of the best moments of my life, but I didn't think it would piss you off."

"I'm not pissed off. What makes you think that?"

Lots, I thought, but I kept my mouth shut. I realized that that moment in Starbucks had been one of my best because it had been unmitigated, and it seems like we don't really get a lot of those in life. Yet that moment had produced a fundamental shift in me. I finally had that boat to cross the pond with. I glanced at Alan again, glowering and pale, and it suddenly struck me that at this point he must have realized he was no longer in the boat with me. He had stuck with me as I weaved and dodged through life, speeding through highway metaphors and ping-ponging ideas of faith back and forth, never really landing anywhere. He liked the Zen-Druid-Rock-Star-Programmer-Dad guy, but seemed to really have a problem with an unhyphenated Christian.

Chapter 15: One Road Home

Yet, we kept going. We could hardly turn back now anyway. We passed through Laramie, stopping only to get gas, and Alan just sat in the car. Outside of Laramie we began climbing into the hills and began to see the outlines of trees that vaguely resembled a forest, leaving behind the rocky terrain at last. The sun had started to set behind us, casting golden rays and making long shadows through the stunted pines around us.

I glanced at Alan from time to time, and with each passing mile he seemed to get paler, as if he were fading away. We spend a lot of time looking at other people's eyes to try and get clues about their thoughts and feelings; how do you read someone whose eyes have nothing to say? Finally, just outside of Cheyenne, I couldn't stand it anymore.

"Hey, Alan. Are you asleep over there?"

"Yes. No. Actually, I'm feeling pretty sick to my stomach."

I laughed a little nervously. "There's a Denny's coming up at the next exit. You want to stop for something?"

Alan's silence couldn't have said *no* any louder had he shouted it out. I was actually getting pretty hungry, but was confident there would be more Denny's down the road.

Unexpectedly, he spoke again as we entered Cheyenne. "I never had connections like those. I did have a life, you know. Most people would say I'd done pretty well, with my so-called disability." His voice was getting weak; he was like a gas tank with a big leak in the side. I was reconsidering the Denny's when he spoke again, "OK. So, as we approach the end of this very lengthy journey, you still haven't answered the fundamental question, the first question I asked back in Troutdale. Why ordination? And, now that I think of

Part III: Counterpoint

it, it's really two questions: how does ordination answer your mother's conundrum about being contemplative and active at the same time? And wait! There's three: why ordination in the United Methodist Church?"

I had to laugh. There was no doubt that the failing state of Alan's body had no effect on his mind. "Wow. OK. I guess you don't need something to eat. Well, let's see . . . Even though I started seminary as a candidate in the United Methodist Church, I didn't really know that much about Methodism. Since I was starting at the fairly advanced age of fifty, I admit I liked their system of guaranteed appointments so that I would have a job when I got out of seminary. And Vivian had been a lifelong Methodist and, in spite of her experience with the UCC, or maybe because of it, she decided to join me in pursuing a career in ministry. By 2008, the kids had grown up and moved away from home, so we decided to sell the house in Forest Grove, return to Colorado and attend seminary at a Methodist sponsored school, the Iliff School of Theology in Denver.

"We managed to rid ourselves of a great deal of stuff, cramming all of our belongings into a 24 foot U-Haul, and in August of 2008 we arrived at Deer Park United Methodist Church outside of Bailey Colorado, and set about stowing away all of our stuff in a parsonage that seemed smaller than the truck. Deer Park had hired me as Choir Director—my last such position!—and we lived in the parsonage that the current pastor wasn't using while we attended classes down the hill in Denver at Iliff. Believe it or not, GE allowed me to continue working remotely and part-time, so the separation from the past life wasn't quite yet complete.

"It was a little odd, returning to school after almost thirty years, and studying a subject for which I felt emotionally well-grounded but intellectually unprepared. Vivian, after all, had spent her whole life in a Christian environment, going to Sunday School and attending Bible studies, and she set about mining and challenging those Iliff professors for every last ounce of knowledge they had. I, who had done none of those things, ended up being mostly a sponge. I wanted to absorb all that I had missed in this subject over the years, and again often felt like an outsider trying to catch up. Iliff's constant drumbeat of liberal progressivism could get annoying, but the professors were excellent at forming theological thinkers and helping me acquire what I was really looking for: the language I needed to express my long-held but generally inarticulate beliefs.

"But to more directly answer your questions, it was also at Iliff that I learned about Methodism, and particularly what distinguishes it from

Chapter 15: One Road Home

other Christian denominations, and even more particularly why God had guided me towards that denomination."

"That's the first time you've mentioned God as a driver on your trajectory."

"The Shooter," I mumbled to myself, and oddly Alan didn't challenge me on it. I continued, full voice, "Part of being uncertain about your faith is hesitancy in using the G-word. *Divine Presence* seems oh so much more Zen-like, more sophisticated and ecumenical. But the truth is, everyday people say God, even if they sometimes mean different things by that word. Part of using language successfully is using the vocabulary of your listener, and most church goers are pretty much just plain folks who say God."

"OK. So what Methodist trajectory had God-The-Divine-Presence set you on?"

"We'll need to start with a little history. Methodism was founded back in the 1700s by two brothers, John and Charles Wesley . . ."

"Hey, wait a minute," Alan interrupted, "isn't *your* brother named Charles?"

"Ironic, isn't it? Another bread crumb?" I asked, mysteriously. Alan just shook his head.

"Anyway, John Wesley was the theologian of the two, while Charles was the poet. John, like his father, was an Anglican priest, but he noticed that most of the Anglican churches were filled with the upper crust of society. Many people who had what we would call blue-collar jobs, or worse, were not welcome. So he developed, along with some others, a *method* for including all of God's children. This started with what was called *field preaching*: literally going out into fields or town squares and preaching the Gospel to any and all who would listen. This got to be immensely popular, and Wesley continued his method into ways in which common people could make a greater commitment to their faith.

"Wesley had grown up in a theological environment that was heavily influenced by Calvinism. This was a theology that stressed predestination and its corresponding assumption of a lack of free will to do anything good. If God had chosen you at the beginning of time, you were in, no questions asked, and if God hadn't chosen you at the beginning of time, you were out, doomed to perish or stay in hell for eternity."

"That doesn't sound very Zen."

"It isn't. Of course, Wesley knew nothing about Zen or eastern religions. He had studied the ancient Christian writers, including Pelagius—that

Part III: Counterpoint

Celtic monk I had encountered in Starbucks—but all he knew about him was from the writings of Augustine, Pelagius's most bitter enemy. In Wesley's day everyone thought there were no surviving documents by Pelagius himself, since the Catholic Church had destroyed all of his writings. In modern times, works by Pelagius or works attributed to him have been unearthed, but even with his limited exposure Wesley discerned correctly that Pelagius wanted nothing to do with Augustine's extreme views on predestination, just as Wesley rejected Calvin's views which were derived from Augustine's. So, Pelagius's views aligned not only with Wesley's views, but also with those of Jacobus Arminius. All three shared similar views on the nature of free will and grace as the drivers for divine-human collaboration in this world—co-creating, to use the modern term."

"Whoa! Hold on there. Are you saying that in John Wesley you got that old Celtic monk and Grandpa Arminius all rolled up into one?"

"Ha!" I laughed. "I might even get ole Uncle Sam the Bishop in here, too!"

In a mock voice Alan grumbled, "Sheesh! We should've gotten a bigger car!"

"Right. So, Wesley being an Arminian saw these aspects of Calvinism as a gross denial of the grace of God, not unlike Pelagius had, so you can see why this stuff appealed to me right off the bat. More connections! And you can see why it might appeal to people who had been shut out of the church by those who considered themselves among the elect, and considered the dirty masses among the doomed.

"Wesley developed a theology of grace that extended well beyond simply opposing Calvinism and predestination. To fully live the life God intended, each person must attend to God's grace within themselves and in relationship with God; and within their relationship with society and the world. He called it Personal Holiness and Social Holiness. Many churches, then and now, really just emphasize Personal Holiness because, if salvation is the goal and you are already saved, then obviously you're done. Some churches just emphasize Social Holiness, believing that salvation is achieved through good works and charity. Wesley was pretty much the first to realize that it is the conjoining of these two that produces *complete* holiness. Wholeness, if you will. He was saying, in an eighteenth century sort of way, that one needs to be in relationship with God personally and communally, inwardly and outwardly."

"Contemplative and active?"

Chapter 15: One Road Home

"You got it. There we go. I perceived Wesleyan theology to be the theological answer to my mom's conundrum. In fact, as I learned more and more about Wesleyan theology, several of the missing pieces—those pieces that connected up with the experiences of my childhood—fell into place. Wesleyan theology was the only place where I had seen this balance between the disciplines that were needed to deepen the relationship and interaction with God, and the impetus to bring that interaction into the world through works of charity and piety. I had come to Wesleyan theology through a back door, if you will, only to discover it satisfied one of the lasting questions I had had for twenty years, ever since my mom died.

"Another piece that fell into place had to do with my lasting concern about Christian Exclusivity. How could I possibly honor my upbringing and the tremendous presence of Suzuki-roshi if becoming a Christian meant I must abandon these precious gifts to a lake of fire? How could a loving God sentence Suzuki-roshi to an eternal hell of torture and suffering? Wesley provided at least a partial answer, and I'm pretty comfortable with extending his answer a little bit to satisfy my concerns. Instead of declaring an absolute and exclusive set of orthodox beliefs for Methodists, Wesley adopted a considerably more open policy. Christians, he said, share a core set of beliefs, but most of the other beliefs and practices are a matter of *opinion* upon which we can respectfully disagree without abandoning our paths within God's grace. Wesley did not advocate for a lowest common denominator amongst Christians, but instead encouraged those who were not following his methods to follow their own with equal passion within the overarching rubric of Christian love.[1] And by the way, just so we're clear, *that* is the central rubric of Christianity."

Alan grunted, "So much for the fleas..."

"Wesley extended this policy to at least some non-Christians as well: those who could not possibly have ever heard of Jesus Christ because of their life circumstances. He called them—and I love this term—the Invincibly Ignorant. He believed that God's universal grace must encompass these people as well, otherwise God could hardly be called fair and just. As for people who might have heard about Jesus Christ but were members of another religion, Wesley was less clear. But if you combine the ideas of a fair, just and loving God with the idea Christ's universal atonement—a bedrock of Arminianism—then it's not too difficult to imagine God's grace lighting the paths of Christ-aware non-Christians as well. At the very least,

---

1. See Wesley's sermon *Catholic Spirit* (Wesley, *John Wesley's Sermons*, 299).

Part III: Counterpoint

Wesleyan theology allows you to leave these things up to God's grace and encourages you to act with loving kindness towards everyone, Christian or not. It also encourages humility in regard to your own relationship with the Divine Presence.

"The third, and I think most important area of concordance with my past was actually pointed out to me by Vivian."

"Ah," Alan sighed, "The Apparition."

"Yeah. I told you she was the smart one. Try to remember all the way back to Oregon when I said that Zen was about practice. In fact Zen, when separated out from Buddhism, has very little to do with beliefs and everything to do with practice—a concept also connected with Pelagius.[2] Zen is the discipline whereby the mind and soul are prepared to join in with enlightenment. *Zazen* is an important practice, but Zen really applies to your whole life and the way you approach the living of your life. Zen guys call it *living right*. In this sense Zen could be absorbed into any religion. You could be a Zen Christian or a Zen Muslim or whatever.

"People unfamiliar with Zen often make the mistake of thinking that enlightenment is the goal of Zen practice. Actually, enlightenment is the result of practice. It is the art of getting in sync with enlightenment, not achieving it. *Zen in The Art of Archery* really makes this point. Using the metaphor, and the reality of archery, the author explains that hitting the target with the arrow is not the goal of practice, it is the result. Achieving perfection in the all-encompassing art of archery will blur the distinctions between archer, arrow, bow and target until all of these distinctions disappear. In that state, the arrow *must* hit the target, for it is one with it. If you substitute your life for archery, then your practice will eventually blur the distinction between *self* and everything else. With the practice of becoming perfect at life—living right—you *must* encounter enlightenment, for you have become one with it.

"What Vivian pointed out is that in a strange, eighteenth century way, Wesley was saying the exact same thing about his method for practicing *perfection*. Many people believe that the goal of Christianity is salvation. Wesley believed that salvation was the work of Jesus Christ, not you or me or anyone else. He exclaimed boldly in one of his sermons 'Ye *are* saved

---

2. Pelagius wrote: "Thus it is not what you believe that matters; it is how you respond with your heart and your actions. It is not believing in Christ that matters; it is becoming like him." Quoted in Newell, *Listening for the Heartbeat*, 12.

Chapter 15: One Road Home

through faith!' quoting Paul from Ephesians.³ But, like the Zen practitioners that he knew nothing about, Wesley believed that we are called to live into that salvation—to get in sync with that salvation—by practicing daily the disciplines that would result in perfection. He called this process *sanctification*. So, salvation is not the goal of Christianity, it is the result of Christian practice. We don't *earn* God's grace; we learn to *participate* with God's grace. A Christian who practices the disciplines of sanctification and moves toward perfection *must* be saved, for he or she has become one with it: the state of perfection.

"And perfection is discovered when the distinctions between Personal Holiness and Social Holiness disappear, making it quite similar to the philosophy of wholeness that you find in Zen. I'm not sure if Wesley ever explicitly outlined this concept in quite this way, but I am certain he would agree with a theology of wholeness; of the blurring of the distinctions between ego/self and the Divine Presence until they disappear. For me, this became an explication in relatively conventional Christian language of the wholeness I had sensed as a child from Suzuki-roshi. It allowed me to close that loop and experience deeply and for the first time the sense that my life didn't have to be one of division. I felt unhyphenated for the first time."

Alan whispered, "And the Apparition thought all that up?"

"Yeah. Not bad for 'undue female influence,' don't you think?"

Alan's voice became so low that I could hardly hear him. "Touché."

He sat quietly for a few minutes and seemed to regain his voice a little. "That's good stuff. I think you almost have me convinced, though I stress the word *almost*. But it sounds as if you really should be a Buddhist-Christian. I know people who call themselves Buddhist-Christians."

"Some people have called that *religious promiscuity*,⁴ though I would only apply that term to people who aren't very serious about the effort. Still, I understand the desire to meld traditions, motivated as I am by trying to make connections. And if you try to combine the two on the level of commonality between the wisdom teachings of the Buddha and the wisdom teachings of the Christ, you do get a lot of value and points of connection.

---

3. See Wesley's sermon *Salvation by Faith* (Wesley, *John Wesley's Sermons*, 39). He was referencing the King James Bible, paraphrasing Ephesians 2:8: "For by grace are ye saved through faith; and that not of yourselves: it is the gift of God." (KJV)

4. Paul Knitter tells a humorous story about religious promiscuity in the conclusion to *Without Buddha I Could Not be a Christian*, but I don't know if he invented the term. He (and others) prefer the term *hybrid* when talking about co-mingling religious traditions.

Part III: Counterpoint

It's a good fit and a great place to explore those common human connections. And there are certainly enough points of connection for Christians and Buddhists to not just get along, but to grow and learn deeply from each other. But I think you can get much more value, and go far deeper, if you ultimately stick to one path."

"How so?"

I sighed. "Look, we would need to keep driving all the way to Florida to get into that. I'll just say that I think people who really want to go deeply into their faith, to go beyond wisdom teachings and into the numinous aspects, would spend a lot of time trying to reconcile metaphysical concepts, like reincarnation versus resurrection, instead of experiencing the mystery of their faith. Too many collisions, too many points of separation, would probably be a distraction rather than an illumination. This separation doesn't invalidate either path, it just means that the path you're on will be much clearer and richer if it is a single path. I think it was Thich Nhat Hanh, the Vietnamese Buddhist, who said you should dig your well in your own backyard. Being a faithful Buddhist or a faithful Christian are both ways to find the deep aquifer of joy that God is streaming beneath all of creation. It seems to me that trying to dig two wells at once is just a lot harder.

"The aquifer is, of course, the mystery; the numinous aspect of the Divine that people of all religions must sooner or later encounter if they have been seeking it. Wesley was, of course, a man of the Age of Reason who did not dwell particularly on the mystical, numinous side of things, but he freely and frequently admitted that God's grace was something we experience every day, but was beyond our ability to explain. We could describe it, but not analyze it. Just like *Jeux* so many years before in music school, the limits of human reason must sooner or later give way to the mystery of faith. Zen is famous for its use of illogic and misdirection in order to point to the numinous; Wesleyan theology does the same as reason, tradition and experience are subsumed in grace. Music too has given me a pathway to the mystery, and these three distinct personalities have produced a kind of theological triple kiss: Music, Zen and Methodism. Weird, huh? But also absolutely fantastic!

"All of this allowed me to authentically dig a well in my own back yard. Although I imagine Wesley might be scandalized by the thought of combining an arcane Asian discipline with his enlightenment era method, within my own experience I discovered I could embrace the embedded religion of my culture wholeheartedly without betraying the spiritual values

Chapter 15: One Road Home

of my upbringing. Zen, Music and Methodism aren't overlaid or force fit into something they are not: each places its distinction upon the palette, which are then combined to create a complete picture. Not fractured, not scattered, but in one piece. Whole."

"But if it's so great, why isn't every Christian a Methodist?"

"You really need to improve your listening skills, Alan! As I have said frequently, the paths that lead to the house of God are as diverse as the people seeking God. The religious buffet is wide and deep, and it is filled with God's grace. Religious diversity doesn't have to be divisive; it can truly be a tremendous gift as people seek the path that best suits their soul. It is also a core principle of Wesley's theology that there are many valid Christian paths. But given my background and upbringing, and the timing, and the people who influenced me, and of course the inexplicable call of grace, it ended up being the right path for me.

"I'm not suggesting that Methodists have found a magic ingredient, or that their institutions aren't subject to the same failings as any other religious institution. But it seems to me that we have invested so much energy in highlighting the institutional flaws that we sometimes forget that the church remains the primary holder of that sacred trust and the primary distributor of Christ's message; a message that still resonates loudly even through our flawed institutions.

"I suspect that many people, including a lot of Methodists, see the United Methodist Church like an old 1965 Dodge Dart: musky, old-fashioned, and out of date. But if you looked beneath the hood you'd discover this shiny, powerful, ageless engine called Wesleyan theology that never runs out of gas."

"OK, now that is just weird."

"Weird or not, the church invests a lot of time and energy in trying to spruce up the exterior, repaint the car, maybe slap on some new tires, when what they really should be doing is jumping in and driving the thing using that ageless engine. Some people recognize this, of course, but it's sometimes an uphill battle to get people to just look under the hood!

"And isn't it ironic that Mom pursued Zen at a home a mile away and was disappointed, and yet there was a Methodist church just down the block! Not that Methodists have always perfectly practiced their own theology, but still ... Wesley wasn't really a contemplative so it's hard to say how he would have felt about Zen. He denounced the *Quietist* movement of his day, but that movement would seem cultish even in our day.[5] The point is, baked into Wesleyan theology are the practices and structures that weave together the elements that so eluded my mom, but are essential to a spiritual practice of wholeness. As Richard Carlson said, 'You become what you practice most.'[6] In a way, you can't really be a Methodist unless you are a Zen Methodist; unless you are someone committed to spiritual practice and growth both inwardly and outwardly, and committed to blurring the lines between the inward and the outward until they disappear. I believe this very Zen idea is exactly what Wesley meant when he talked about perfection. Or, Paul again: '. . . when perfection comes, the imperfect disappears.'"[7]

Alan seemed completely lost, and my quote from 1 Corinthians didn't even solicit a sarcastic grunt. Instead, he finally said weakly, "What about Druid? I really liked Druid. You linked up Zen, music and Christianity, but you left out Druid."

I pursed my lips and said, "You know, just like my Zen-essence didn't arise out of Wesleyan theology, my Druid-essence didn't either. Wesley had a scientific rather than a mystical approach to nature and creation. Nevertheless, he considered nature and the natural world a revelation of God,[8] and God's all-encompassing grace, which he called *prevenient* grace, extended to all of creation. He would have objected to a pagan-ish worship of nature itself *as* God, but he would have accepted the idea of nature being *imbued* with God, just as my Druid-essence does.

"Still, all of the themes we've beaten to death on this trip started out like colors on an artist's palette, but somehow came together on a canvas as a whole and complete picture. Think of something like Monet's *The Japanese Footbridge*. Every color started out as a separate blob on the palette, yet with each brush stroke each color is ultimately subsumed within the whole painting. Scrutinizing this painting with a microscope would be pointless. Even though we know that each individual brush stroke is there, the picture makes no sense unless viewed as a whole. So I'm not trying to shoehorn

---

5. The Quietists, founded in the 1670s, believed that a perfect union with God could only be achieved through contemplative practice, an idea clearly antithetical to Wesley's method of sanctification.

6. Carlson, "Priority Management".

7. 1 Corinthians 13:10 (NIV)

8. See Wesley, *A Survey of the Wisdom of God in the Creation*.

Chapter 15: One Road Home

spiritual naturalism into Wesleyan theology; instead I have discovered that there is room for it on the palette used for my own painting."

I paused for a moment, then said tentatively, "Uh . . . sorry about the visual metaphor."

Alan was getting further and further away, and he spoke in a dreamy voice, "Hmm? What? I, uh . . . Don't worry. I didn't go blind until I was twenty-three." And then, even further away, if that was possible, "I actually saw a Monet once in the Portland Art Museum." Then perking up, he added, "Besides, Monet himself was nearly blind when he painted that thing."

I was flabbergasted. The last thing I thought would reach Alan was a visual metaphor. In the wistfulness of his voice, I thought I could hear an unrequited dream of becoming Monet; yet Monet had not been deterred by his advancing cataracts, something that Alan seemed to both identify with, and despise.

"Well," I said at last, "on my canvas, the question arises: how can you be whole with God if you are separated from God's creation? I guess it's possible, but it makes no sense. In the end, I guess nature is linked to the rest of, well, everything, by its participation in the mystery. God in the meadow at Pinecrest or the Welsh stone circle can be experienced, but not really explained. Described, but not analyzed. Everything we've talked about on this long trip—Zen, music, nature, Christianity, relationships, snails, churches, life, death—would by themselves be monochromatic blobs on a palette; but together they have created a beautiful portrait of the mystery. The mystery: that numinous experience of something far greater than ourselves, yet inextricably intertwined with all things. Wesley might call it 'prevenient grace.' Intellectual Christians might say 'simultaneously transcendent and imminent.' Buddhists might say 'one with everything.' I might paraphrase Monet's contemporary Debussy by saying, 'without mystery, there is nothing.'"

Alan was fading out, as if he were on a dimmer switch that only went down. I reached into the back seat and grabbed the bag of cheap cookies and put them in Alan's lap.

"You gotta eat something, man. You're about ready to evaporate."

He pawed at the cookies without complaint and stuck a few in his mouth, leaving crumbs all over the passenger seat. After a minute he seemed to perk up a little, but again I wondered just how much I had said really meant anything to him. I wondered, unfairly, if being blind blinded

Part III: Counterpoint

him to grace as well. Perhaps not literally—I knew other, very grace-filled blind people—but metaphorically it seemed to fit.

"Well," he finally said, "I . . . I don't know. We've come a great distance, both in years and miles. Lots of stuff . . . lots of stuff . . . I am defeated . . ."

"Alan, for goodness' sake, don't . . ."

"I have but a single arrow left in my quiver," he said, suddenly dramatic, but then pathetically weak. "Have you really answered the very first question, the one I asked all the way back in Troutdale: why this ordination crap? All that you've told me, all of your beliefs and desires, could be implemented in other ways, couldn't they? Do you really need the imprimatur of a big institution to legitimize all of this?"

In spite of my words and passion, Alan still could not bring himself to trust the church. While I could understand his truculence, he was without any foundation of faith. Under these circumstances, could I really explain trust?

"No Alan. It's not about legitimization, and it's not very much about the big institution, which ultimately is no more and no less than another means of grace. There's a very, very big difference between not walking away from something and walking towards it. Between skating on the surface of the ice or falling through and really starting to swim. Between driving back and forth on the same stretch of freeway over and over again, or getting off on the side roads to see what's really going on. It's about trusting the Shooter." Alan looked puzzled, unaware of my inner-Longmire, but I continued. "Safety and risk aversion and timidity are comfortable, but not meaningful. It's the difference between survival and living—truly living. After surviving cancer, I really wanted to live, and this path opened up before me, including the big institution, and I decided to risk taking it. You could say it was unbidden, it was certainly unexpected, but it was a trajectory I'd been on my whole life and I didn't even know it. All the various tea leaves blended to make a unique cup of tea. All the colors on the palette combined to make one whole picture. All the themes harmonized to create a single song. All the roads converged to make one road home." Now it was my turn to be far away. "So, yeah, on Saturday, God willing, I am going to be ordained, just like ole Uncle Sam the Bishop. It's not because I need a stamp of approval or institutional legitimacy. It's because I want to fall through the ice. I am choosing not to live on a cold, hard, flat surface."

We began the long slow southerly curve as we merged from eastbound I-80 to southbound I-25, and in a few minutes crossed over the Colorado

Chapter 15: One Road Home

border. Out of Wyoming at last, I thought. But we seemed to have turned a metaphorical corner as well, and Alan sat in silence as we motored south through Fort Collins and Longmont. I had to admit to myself, considering how much I had talked along this trip, that silence felt pretty good. I could say a few more things, I guess, but Alan had sunk into his own, feverish world, and I assumed he was just trying to absorb all that we had spoken of. Or was he working on actively rejecting all that we had spoken of? If this was going to produce another acerbic outburst, it certainly was a long time coming.

And in fact, it never came. I finally realized that Alan had been asleep since about Loveland. As we approached Denver, I finally activated the GPS system in the rental car and punched in Alan's new address. We exited the freeway at last and wound through various streets and intersections until finally turning off onto a quiet, tree-lined street. I gently nudged Alan as I pulled up to his apartment building.

"We're here. Time to see your new home."

Alan rolled out of the car and stood up stiffly, then clumsily reached back into the front seat for his cane. The light from the streetlamp didn't improve his pallor, and he just stood there at the curb, having no idea where to go or what to do. I wondered if he was going to throw up. I grabbed one of his bags and guided him up the walk. He handed me a key attached to an oversized paper clip with a sticky-note augured through it with the apartment number, and I unlocked the door and led/pushed Alan in. His apartment was on the ground floor, and as we tumbled in I noticed it was completely empty. Barren. Alan's furniture from Portland hadn't arrived yet.

"Are you going to be alright, man? There's nothing here."

"Just grab the sleeping bag. I'll hang out here alone—thank God—until morning. Look around for me, will you, and see if there's a grocery store or a place to eat nearby."

I went back out to the car and looked up towards the main street we had come off of, but there was just a strip mall with a book store and a dry cleaner. I turned around and noticed that, two blocks down, there was another cross street and on the corner there appeared to be—oh no, it couldn't be—but yes, there it was: a Denny's.

There was no way I was going to mention this to Alan, so I grabbed the rest of his bags, the sleeping bag, and the stale cookies, and lugged them all back into the apartment. When I got back, he was already dozing off, and after a very brief conversation that thankfully didn't include food, I finally abandoned him as he lay curled up on the floor.

Part III: Counterpoint

Once again I awoke with a start, finding myself still on the back porch of the cabin in Bailey. It was very late and the moon had set. The trees no longer cast pale shadows; they were now just dark shadows themselves. Vivian, always the night owl, was still on the sofa inside reading and the light from her reading lamp spilled out meekly onto a little patch of the back porch. For a moment I couldn't remember how I'd gotten there, and I thought *how did I get on to the porch at Pinecrest?* But after a moment I got my bearings, enough to feel that wave of peace that can only come about when you know you are at home. *The minute I stepped into the room, I knew I had come home.* Mom's words echoed around in my head. But then a much more ominous thought popped into my mind: *Alan is still alive!* As much as I had awoken that morning not wanting to know, I knew.

In our drowsy conversation before I left his apartment, we agreed to meet on Saturday just before the ordination service at the Starbucks on Arapahoe. *Do you want me to pick you up?* I had asked him. *No,* he replied in a whisper, *I'll take a bus or a cab.*

Frankly, he had looked like death not even warmed over, and I doubted he would show up at all. *Maybe his fate didn't matter after all,* I thought hopefully, but was not really able to truly convince myself.

Postlude

Before ordination, chop wood, carry water.
After ordination, chop wood, carry water.

—VARIATION ON AN OLD CHINESE PROVERB

Chapter 16: Starbucks

As expected, Thursday and Friday at Annual Conference went according to plan. Go here, dress up in this, go there, say this whether you mean it or not, get your picture taken: *smile*! No matter how idealistic one might be, the institution will exact its price. Vivian and I did almost everything together, which made it all so much easier, and on Friday evening we were both voted in to the Order of Elders by our fellow clergy. This is a little bit like getting the marriage license; ordination is the wedding.

Things really didn't slow down on Saturday morning, with rehearsals and more pictures, but around 1 p.m. we had a scheduled break, and I said to Vivian, "Let's go up to the Starbucks on Arapahoe."

"You go ahead," she said. "I'll drop you off and go do some shopping and meet you back there."

"OK."

I entered the Starbucks as Vivian drove away, and couldn't help but think of that Starbucks in Salem where old Pelagius and Celtic spirituality had blown through me. It seemed a little bizarre to have so many major life events take place in Denny's and Starbucks. Life on the road, I guess.

I scanned the room, but there was no sign of Alan. I smiled to myself, guiltily thinking how easy it would be if he just sort of slid out of my life. Who needs closure, anyway? I ordered a Caramel Macchiato from the barista and sat down at a little table facing the door. I had barely settled in when there he was, fumbling with the front door, his cane wildly whipping about for a moment until he got his bearings and stumbled through the door. He stopped for a moment as the door shut behind him, and for an instant I could swear he was actually looking for me.

Postlude

He looked terrible. He still had on the clothes he had worn the last day in the car, and though I think he might have showered a few times, he had a greasy, unkempt look and wild hair. His pale skin was almost transparent, and the only color on his face beside his straggly beard came from the ubiquitous aviators that he wore. It was pathetic, especially in contrast to the always natty dresser and impeccably groomed man I had known in Portland. And, in spite of my fantasies, he really couldn't see me, or anything else, and was just waiting impatiently for direction.

"I'm over here, Alan!" I shouted out across the room. Would he be angrier if I got up and guided him, or left him to his own devices? By the time I had made up my mind, he was feeling for the chair across from me. I wasn't certain, but it seemed like he smelled somewhat like rotten fish.

"Hey man," I said with false jollity, "it's good to see you. Wasn't sure you were going to make it."

"I'm going back to Portland," he said without preamble, "and order me a soy latte."

"What!"

"S-o-y l-a-t-t-e."

"No, no, Portland. I mean . . . I mean . . . You just got here."

"The furniture truck showed up on Friday, and I just sent 'em back. They were reeeeeeeally pissed, but a blind guy can get a lot done by looking pathetic. I'm going to have to pay for it myself, but it's worth it."

"I . . . I'm . . . I don't know what to say. Do you . . . do you have a job? Can you still live in your old apartment?"

"Fortunately, they still wanted me at the old job. There's a real advantage to not burning bridges when subsequent events don't turn out as planned. And I wrangled a different apartment in the same building, which will make it easier for the movers."

"Well, I'm . . . I'm flabbergasted. You took a real risk coming out here; threw everything up in the air. And now you're going back, just like that. Why?"

"Because all of your jabbering made me realize what I wanted was to be safe, comfortable and risk averse," he said, coldly. "I want to stay on the ice, thank you very much."

We both could sense that the divide was widening, but I soldiered on. "I, uh, don't suppose you want me to drive you back?"

"Dear God in heaven, no! I doubt I would survive the trip. No, I'm flying out tomorrow morning."

Chapter 16: Starbucks

"Do you need a ride to the airport?"

"For God's sake, STOP IT! Stop lying to me! Stop pretending you're anything but ecstatic to see me go!" Alan caught himself and breathed a little. "Besides, your precious Rocky Mountains are killing me. There's no air up here. If I breathe any more pollen I'm going to turn into a pine cone. No, this way I can flee safely back into the past. I can haunt your memories and wake you up at 3 a.m. with guilt and regrets. You can imagine me basking in the rain and roses of Portland, while I can imagine you gasping for air as you sink under the ice." He paused, and then whispered almost to himself, "I suspect we'd both be wrong."

Another long silence ensued. I never had ordered his latte, but he seemed unconcerned. Finally I said, "I'm happy you're going. I'm glad you're going. But I'm not ecstatic. It's not like I'm throwing away something valueless, some piece of trash. But when you walk towards something new, you inevitably walk away from the old, and you can't just keep turning around and looking back all the time." I too paused for a moment, then said, "Hey. What do you think? Do you think you could come to the ordination ceremony tonight?"

Alan softly, gently, shook his head. "No."

"Why not?"

"Look at you, my Zen-Druid-bodhisattva-Methodist friend. You are going someplace where I can't follow. You're full of hope and optimism. I am not. You think that your whole life has led up to this point, whereas my life is going where it's always gone: nowhere. You believe in something larger than yourself, and I barely believe in myself at all. Your palette is full of vibrant colors; mine is simply smears of grey and black." He paused for a moment, then added for emphasis, "Monochromatic blobs."

At least Alan hadn't lost his sense of drama. He felt around on the table for the non-existent coffee cup, then sighed when he realized it was never coming. "Do you remember that movie *Signs*?" I nodded. "Remember that scene with Mel Gibson and Joaquin Phoenix, where Gibson says there are two types of people? One type believes that things happen for a reason, so that when desperate times come they are filled with hope and faith, believing that all things have a purpose? The other type believes the universe is random, and things just happen through pure luck. When desperate times come, they are filled with fear and doubt, because they just don't know how their luck will turn out." Alan slowly began rising from the table. "One

Postlude

person can't be both types of people at the same time. You have no more use for me."

Alan slowly got up and began limping towards the door. I watched him go with sadness and guilty relief. Suddenly, he turned and, taking off his aviators, he stared right at me with such intensity I again could have sworn he could see me.

"You didn't really want to kill me, did you?"

It seemed as if we locked eyes for a few seconds, and I didn't dare move, I didn't dare twitch. But mostly, I didn't dare answer his question. After a moment, he lowered his piercing blind gaze and put on his aviators once again.

"Just remember one thing, John. I made you who you are."

He turned and made his way out the door, fading rapidly into the late afternoon sun. I never saw him again.

Chapter 17: Beginner's Mind

ON THAT SATURDAY EVENING when Vivian and I were ordained, a lot of people died. I vaguely remember the District Superintendent calling out my name, and as I stepped out on to the chancel, I couldn't help but look around one last time for Alan, even though I knew he was gone for good. I stepped forward and knelt in front of the Bishop. Even as she laid her hands on me, I realized she had no clue about the corpses that were lying all around us. That old adult child of an alcoholic breathed his last uncertain breath, and as he died he took with him all of those years wasted on self-recrimination, guilt, regret and doubt. They went as quietly as Dad had years before, a ghost booted out by the Holy Ghost, you might say. I suppose that particular demon might return unbidden from time to time, carrying with it the temptation to blame everything that's bad in my life on my father and his addictive behavior, but, like a toothless rattlesnake, its boozy ravings will no longer hold any power. The "World's Greatest Musician" also lay in repose, eternally sleeping in 5/8 time. He really wanted the fame, wanted to be talked about in the same breath as either Paul McCartney or Luciano Pavarotti, depending on the era. Without the glamor and glitz of a professional career, I got the opportunity to really fall in love with music, to experience its joy and to be a servant to its mystery. And Mom finally died, too. Her dying voice, wistfully regretting something she could not find, had launched me on to the winding path that had led to this night. But her journey finally ended here; I was no longer on a borrowed path. The impetus to find a union of contemplation and action had been satisfied, and had been returned back to Mom as a parting gift: the path was fully my own now.

Postlude

And of course, there was Alan, the man I could have become. Not bad, but not good, not unhappy, but not happy, simultaneously blind and insightful. A hyphenated man. Thinking of him reminded me of all of those moments in life when the smallest of choices changed everything, sometimes unknowingly and often beyond our control. All of the what-ifs that could have resulted in a different life: what if Vivian had chosen to stay home from that audition way back in San Jose? What if Mom had chickened out on connecting with Suzuki-roshi and the Haiku Zendo? What if I had relentlessly pursued my singing career, family be damned. Perhaps then Alan might not have needed to go back to Portland. In fact, he probably never would have left.

I knew his last words to me were true. I couldn't be me without him. But if we are to take seriously the transformative power of the Spirit Life, Alan's departure was inevitable; it is the very definition of transformation. Life isn't a zero-sum game where you have to give up something in order to get something—Alan had been right about that, too—but still, no matter how good and right the new is, transformation always involves loss. But not death: Alan really couldn't die. As the Bishop intoned the final words of consecration and I shakily stood up, I knew that Alan—or his ghost, anyway—had been ordained too.

Vivian was ordained right after me, and I realized that she probably had a lot of ghosts with her, too. As she rose from the kneeler and I placed her stole— the symbol of ordination—over her shoulders as she had placed mine upon me, I looked around and for a moment heard a giant *whoosh!* I realized it was the sound of all of those ghosts leaving the sanctuary forever, free at last.

In their place was the heartbeat of new life all around me. My colleagues, twelve others who were also being ordained on that evening, gathered around as each of us went through the brief consecration by the Bishop. *Not a single Mr. Hyde among 'em,* I thought. Some were young, some were starting out somewhat later in life like Vivian and me, but I felt strongly that all of us represented the hope and mystery that I had so perilously embraced. I was certain that they too had all brought ghosts with them, and for a moment I imagined a confused and raucous confab of dislocated spirits taking place above us. But no, they were gone. Whatever metaphor my colleagues had chosen, I suspected all of them understood that they were falling through the ice. We had all chosen to walk towards something, with absolutely no clue whatsoever what the road would look

Chapter 17: Beginner's Mind

like or where it would lead. And none of us could escape the journey metaphor. Like Frodo, we were all on a path that leads away from self-interest in order to serve a higher purpose and nurture a sacred trust. The church has reinvented itself hundreds of times in the centuries since the disciples were commissioned, and for all of my misgivings over the years it felt hopeful to not be falling through the ice alone.

And those precious connections with the past that I had longed for were there too. Uncle Bill and Aunt Maggie were there, the last of that generation of my family. Two of my cousins attended as well, reminding me that no matter how old we got we would always be at heart teenagers at Pinecrest. I realized that the guilt list had become a ghost as well. *Let the dead bury the dead* . . . Hattie Lou had flown out from California with her husband, and it was she who brought the stole up onto the chancel for Vivian to place on me. When she gave it to Vivian to put on my shoulders, I wondered, had Mom been present, would she have needed to suck on a lifesaver to keep from laughing? I think not, but it would have been wonderful to see if I could have ever gotten her to attend a Methodist church. She hadn't known it, but I think maybe she was a Zen Methodist, too.

My oldest son Jonathan was there with his wife, and my other son Jeffrey had flown all the way out from Portland—yes, Portland—to be there as well. All of them looked proud and a little confused. They will find their own paths, or perhaps more poignantly, their paths will find them. From our children we learn to embrace our future; from the past we learn to embrace our children.

After the service and the hoopla-party that followed, Vivian and I, along with our boys, drove back up the hill to the cabin in Bailey, where we celebrated some more before retiring at a very late hour to our beds. But I was still too wound up, too full of emotion and wonder, and while Vivian prepared for bed, I once again went out on to the back porch to decompress and commune with the trees, as I had done so often for so many years at Pinecrest. What did it all mean?

At the clergy session on the Friday before the ordination service, each candidate for ordination gave an obligatory three minute "speech" to introduce themselves to the collection of Elders and Deacons from around the conference. A part of mine went like this:

> The wisest person I had ever met in person, Shunryu Suzuki-roshi, once said, "In the beginner's mind there are many possibilities, in

Postlude

the expert's mind there are few." And the wisest person ever once said, "I will make all things new again."

No doubt most in attendance understood this in the context of my impending ordination, though I doubt anyone there except Vivian understood this in the larger context of my life. Suzuki-roshi stood as a *koan* in my life, a model of a soul deeply rooted yet open to the movement of all possibilities, so it seemed fitting to set a Beginner's Mind as the theme for my ministry. Like hitting the target in archery, it is not the goal, it is the result of practice, discipline and detachment from self-interest. These sound like very Zen concepts, and they are, but they are also very Christian concepts. I really liked that.

As I sat on my back porch pondering these weighty philosophical matters, I knew that Alan was right about one more thing: I wouldn't be immune from 3 a.m. regrets and the occasional rehashing of every stupid thing I had done in my life. But the attitude of Beginner's Mind suggests that these, like the past itself, are only tethered ghosts, messy and annoying; a night of rest at a good angle of repose will chase them away each morning. As I listened to the gentle wind play music on the boughs of the pines, I felt affirmed, connected. I felt unhyphenated, and for the first time in my life, authentic. Zen, Druid, Musician, Father, Husband, Pastor, Christian, Methodist—the list could go on for some time—but whatever these things are they are me all together—not in pieces—wrapped within the Divine Presence. I felt whole. I was tempted for a moment to grab my iPod and listen to Debussy's *Jeux*, but the evening was too warm and the stars too inviting: no need to add mystery to mystery. Instead, as I sat under the crystalline Colorado sky, I found myself recalling the rest of the poem that had come to me in the Safeway parking lot, eons ago.

Chapter 17: Beginner's Mind

Here inside the earthbent edge of heaven,
Within the span of endless sage and sky,
Where clear-eyed dreamers toiled
We wait. Remembering.

Where distance melts the miles into days
And dreams expand to meet the far horizon,
A point of intersection in the vastness,
A gathering in of heart and mind.

Anchored deep to rock that spirit lives.
Still firm in our directions, undiminished.
Borderland between the past and future.
Inheritors in the promised land.[1]

The sun will rise tomorrow morning over Long Scraggy Peak, and I will enjoy one more day of sacred nothing before getting on the road again in ministry, firm in my direction. But in one piece . . . in one piece, a spirit anchored deep to rock yet free to begin anew. A heart gathered in. Amen.

---

1. (Carwin, *Borderland*, st. 3-5)

Acknowledgments

You would think that writing an autobiography would be sort of a solo affair, but in fact I have received help from a number of people. I would like to thank the folks who waded through the first drafts of the work and helped so much in straightening things out: Steven Lewis, author of *Landscape as Sacred Space: Metaphors for the Spiritual Journey* who began mentoring me at The Northwest House of Theological Studies and inspired me by calling himself a "type A contemplative." Rita Berglund is my spiritual director, who nursed me through those nervous months leading up to ordination and who helped tremendously in the "gathering in of heart and mind."

Although we never met, I would like to acknowledge the influence of the late Gerald May. He was one of Vivian's teachers at the Shalem Institute, but his book *The Wisdom of Wilderness* is not only full of wisdom, it also gave me a pattern for drawing meaning out of life's experiences. I think he was a real *bodhisattva*.

I would also like to thank my pantheon of spiritual heroes: Rev. Edwin C. Coon, Rev. Gwendolyn Drake, Revs. Mark & Cheryl Goodman-Morris, Rev. Deb Olyenik and of course Shunryu Suzuki-roshi. I didn't get where I got by myself.

It would require an additional book to acknowledge the help, support, loving criticism, patience and encouragement from my wife of twenty-nine years, Vivian Hiestand. I very much doubt I could have gotten through the ordination process without her, and most definitely would never have even started this book. Heck, I can't even get through a day without her.

Bibliography

Bourgeault, Cynthia. *The Wisdom Jesus: Transforming Heart and Mind—A New Perspective on Christ and His Message.* Boston: Shambhala, 2011.

Carlson, Richard. "Priority Management-You Become What You Practice Most." http://infonet.prioritymanagement.com/index.php?section_copy_id=9815&section_id=1187.

Carwin, Marilyn J. *Borderland.* Fleming, CO: Unpublished, 1987.

Chadwick, David. *Crooked Cucumber: the Life and Zen teaching of Shunryu Suzuki.* New York: Broadway, 1999.

———. Hiestand, Barbara, ed. "Haiku Zendo - Stories of Shunryu Suzuki Roshi." http://www.cuke.com/Cucumber%20Project/suzuki%20stories/haiku1.html.

Downing, Michael. *Shoes Outside the Door: Desire, Devotion, and Excess at San Francisco Zen Center.* Washington D.C.: Counterpoint, 2001.

Hagiya, Grant. *Spiritual Kaizen.* Nashville: Abingdon, 2013.

Herrigal, Eugen. *Zen in the Art of Archery.* Pantheon Books/Random House, 1953.

Johnson, Craig. *The Cold Dish: A Walt Longmire Mystery.* New York: Penguin Group US, 2004.

Knitter, Paul F. *Without Buddha I Could Not Be a Christian.* London: OneWorld, 2009.

Lewis, Steven. *Landscape as Sacred Space: Metaphors For the Spiritual Journey.* Eugene: Cascade, 2005.

May, Gerald. *The Wisdom of Wilderness.* New York: HarperCollins, 2006.

Newell, J. Phillip. *Listening for the Heartbeat of God.* Mahwah: Paulist, 1997.

Pirsig, Robert. *Zen And the Art of Motorcycle Maintenance.* New York: Bantam/William Morrow, 1974.

Rees, B.R. *Pelagius: Life and Letters.* Woodbridge: Boydell, 1988.

Roberts, Bernadette. *The Path to No-Self.* Boston: Shambhala, 1985.

———. *What is Self?* Boulder: Sentient, 2005.

Suzuki, Shunryu. *Zen Mind, Beginner's Mind.* Boston: Weatherhill, 1973.

Tolkien, J. R. R. *The Lord of the Rings.* Boston: Houghton Mifflin, 1965.

Watts, Alan. *The Way of Zen.* New York: Pantheon, 1957.

Wesley, John. *John Wesley's Sermons: An Anthology.* Edited by Albert C. Outler and Richard Heitzenrater. Nashville: Abingdon, 1991.

———. "A Survey of the Wisdom of God in the Creation: A Compendium of Natural Philosophy in Two Volumes." http://wesley.nnu.edu/john-wesley/a-compendium-of-natural-philosophy.

www.ingramcontent.com/pod-product-compliance
Lightning Source LLC
Chambersburg PA
CBHW051932160426
43198CB00012B/2125